LUXURY
DREAM HOMES

HOME PLANNERS

LUXURY DREAM HOMES

Published by Home Planners, LLC
Wholly owned by Hanley-Wood, LLC
3275 West Ina Road, Suite 110
Tucson, Arizona 85741

Distribution Center:
29333 Lorie Lane
Wixom, Michigan 48393

Jan Prideaux, Editor In Chief
Marian E. Haggard, Editor
Nick Nieskes, Plans Editor
Chester E. Hawkins, Graphic Designer
Peter Zullo, Graphic Production Artist

Photo Credits
Front & Back Covers: Andrew D. Lautman

10 9 8 7 6 5 4 3 2 1

Printed in the United States of America

Library of Congress Catalog Card Number: 2001086996
ISBN softcover: 1-881955-87-7

TABLE OF CONTENTS

ON THE FRONT AND BACK COVERS:

Fine brick detailing, graceful shapes and thoughtful features combine to make this fine five-bedroom home (Design HPT290043) a true showpiece. For more information about this design, please see page 51.

WHAT *is* LUXURY?

SINCE THIS BOOK carries the title, Luxury Dream Homes, a very appropriate question might be: "What exactly is luxury?" Attempting to define luxury may be as difficult as trying to explain dream, the other adjective in the title. One person's dream may be another person's nightmare and consequently "luxury" to one may be simply "getting by" to someone else. But, regardless, certain standards were applied when choosing the designs for this book.

— SIZE —

The houses in this book range from 2,226 to 6,421 square feet. While size alone does not guarantee luxury, in general luxury houses are more expansive than average because it takes more room to include more amenities. Therefore, by any standards, the 5,385-square-foot Victorian by Home Planners on page 69 is a BIG luxury house. Arranged in this commodious space are five bedrooms and four fireplaces, plus a gathering room, game room, dining room, breakfast room, butler's pantry, library, study, etc. As this plan demonstrates, there is no substitute for space.

However, living can also be luxurious in a smaller, more compactly designed space. Witness the 2,957-square-foot Brick Colonial by Design Basics, Inc. on page 25. This four-bedroom, 4½-bath home sports a separate den with a bay window and wet bar, a great room with a cathedral ceiling and fireplace, a formal dining room and an octagonal breakfast room. The master suite includes a ten-foot ceiling and a private bath with a whirlpool tub, shower and huge closet. No matter how you cut it, this home showers its owners with luxurious amenities.

— SCALE AND VOLUME—

Another factor related to size, but quite different in its way, is the scale or volume of a house. Normally, we associate luxury with large or even grand scale, but sometimes good designers can trick our eye into believing that a home is bigger or more grand than it actually is.

Design Basics, Inc. and the Fillmore Design Group exhibit this with homes that allude to a grand scale with smaller square footages. With sweeping roof heights and grand detail, both Plan HPT290134 on page 146 and HPT200135 on page 147 bear a palatial sense within more average-sized plans.

— ARCHITECTURAL DRAMA —

Luxury housing is almost always associated with custom design, meaning that a truly fine, upscale house is usually custom-designed for its site. However, in this book, we've purposefully selected a number of plans that have very interesting architectural features and will add drama to virtually any piece of property.

IF YOU HAVE BUILT

castles in the air,

your work

need not be lost;

that is where

they should be...

Now put the foundations

under them.

– Henry David Thoreau

Worthy of note are the designs by Dan F. Sater of The Sater Design Collection. Plans such as HPT290118 on page 129 and HPT290123 on page 134 encompass a variety of architectural elements that speak to a grandeur and presence usually found only in custom designs. Full walls of windows, dramatic rooflines and octagonal projections permit unique facades and timeless elegance.

— ATTENTION TO DETAIL —

In many cases, the difference between an outstanding house and a so-so house is not size, siting or even style. It's the attention to detail given by the designer and the craftspeople who build it. This most often shows up in exterior ornamentation, especially windows, cornice work and entry details, as well as fine interior work.

Two quite divergent but equally detail-minded designers are Stephen Fuller of Stephen Fuller, Inc. in Atlanta and Robert Fillmore of Fillmore Design Group in Oklahoma City. A recognized name in the stock plan business, Stephen Fuller captures the public's fancy with a series of beautifully ornamented, European-inspired homes. Some of these plans, such as HPT290036 on page 44, appear as if they've been transported directly from the grand country of France and are reminiscent of the finest Old World craftsmanship.

Fillmore Design Group, with its interesting blend of classical details and traditional building materials, makes impressive statements with brick, stone and stucco homes. Notice the finely detailed dentils and pillars of Plan HPT290004 on page 11, which, in spite of its Southern Colonial heritage, could be perfectly at home in the woods of the north.

— OUTSTANDING INTERIOR AMENITIES —

Although we've been talking mainly about exterior features thus far, probably the most distinguishing characteristic of an upscale home is the extra amenities it offers inside. Few people would dispute the need to give special attention to key rooms to make a house luxurious.

One of the most sought-after features in a fine home is a large, well-appointed master suite. Nothing speaks opulence more than the ability to retire to your own private oasis of comfort. Most of the homes in this book were chosen with this in mind. However, a few are worth pointing out as exceptional examples. Notice the superb seclusion offered by Home Planners Plan HPT290043 on page 51 with its self-contained spa/exercise area, bath, shower, His and Hers closets and master bedroom with beehive fireplace. Or the secluded reading room, exceptional layout and private deck of Sater Design Collection's Plan HPT290128 on page 139. Or the gracious formality and elegance of Fillmore Design Group's Plan

BEAUTIFUL BUILDINGS

are more than scientific.

They are true organisms,

spiritually conceived;

works of art, using

the best technology

by INSPIRATION

rather than the

idiosyncrasies

of mere taste

or any averaging

by the committee mind.

– Frank Lloyd Wright

HPT290032 on page 40, with its vaulted bath and private sitting room—complete with fireplace.

Another area that must be blue-ribbon quality in a luxury home is the kitchen/family or kitchen/entertainment areas. With much of family life centered around the kitchen—and with weekends spent entertaining and cooking for guests—this area of the home has become larger, more versatile and more accessible to all members of the household, including visitors.

Consequently, designers are giving much more attention to superbly functional and aesthetically pleasing kitchens. Witness Home Planners outstanding kitchen/family room/living room grouping for Plan HPT290115 on page 126. Or Home Design Service's beautiful octagonal dining room/nook/island kitchen combination for Plan HPT290157 on page 170.

Another space that sets off a luxury home—in fact, heralds it to arriving guests—is the formal entry or foyer. In recent years, this area has returned to a position of prominence and more fanfare is being given to foyers, staircases and the "grand first impression."

Home Design Services offer houses that are studies in entrance one-up-manship. Notice the majestic columns and arched transom foyer of Plan HPT290157. Witness also the grand volume foyers and entrance-making staircases in designs by Alan Mascord Design Associates. Plan HPT290161 and Plan HPT290162 on pages 174-175 are fine examples.

THE FOOLISH MAN

seeks happiness in

the distance...

the wise grows it

under his feet

– James Oppenheim

There are other elements that make certain plans luxurious by nature—some not as grand or immediately apparent as the ones cited above. As examples, consider the handy butler's pantry in Home Planners Plan HPT290065 on page 74; or the game room—complete with built-in shelves, walk-in toy closet, sink and refrigerator area—in Larry E. Belk's Plan HPT290074 on page 84. These are design touches that will prove their value day after day.

Last but not least, as an exercise in pure luxury, study Sater Design collection's Plan HPT290122 on page 133. Nothing is forgotten by way of luxurious detail, from built-ins to planters, lanais to the living-room wet bar. An amenity-laden master suite features a bayed sitting area with a fireplace and outdoor access. Extras include a study, a spacious leisure room and an outdoor kitchen.

Much more could be written about what makes these plans luxurious. But, by now, we're sure you have your own ideas. It's your turn to leaf through these pages, find you own definition of luxury and decide which house is right for you.

HISTORY HAS A WAY OF REPEATING ITSELF,

which, when it comes to architectural styles, can be a good thing. The tried

and true details of the Georgian style—such as corner pilasters and dormer

windows, the stately grace of Greek Revival columns, Doric, Ionic and

Corinthian, and the low-pitched rooflines and high ceilings of Federal-style

homes—all work well in today's architectural version of luxury. History

even affects interior details and the number of amenities. The portico,

transom windows, number of fireplaces and of course the aforementioned

high ceilings can all combine to add style and grace to today's homes. In

this section we show that history doesn't have to be worn out and dusty,

it can give the feeling of strength, beauty and lasting tradition instead.

SHOWN ABOVE:

DESIGN HPT290013 BY

DESIGN BASICS, INC.

SEE PAGE 20 FOR MORE

INFORMATION ON THIS

BEAUTIFUL SOUTHERN

COLONIAL HOME.

HISTORIC INDULGENCE

DESIGN FEATURES

BEDROOMS: 4

BATHROOMS: 3

FIRST FLOOR: 2,253 Sq. Ft.

SECOND FLOOR: 890 Sq. Ft.

TOTAL: 3,143 Sq. Ft.

WIDTH: 61'-6" DEPTH: 64'-0"

DESIGN HPT290001
©ARCHIVAL DESIGNS, INC.

THIS GRAND GEORGIAN HOME begins with a double-door entry topped by a beautiful arched window. Inside, the foyer opens to the two-story living room, which presents a wide bow window overlooking the rear property. Double doors open to a study warmed by a fireplace. The kitchen features a walk-in pantry and serves both the formal dining room and the breakfast area, which adjoins the bright keeping room. The master suite, secluded on the first floor, is large and opulent. Three more bedrooms and two baths are upstairs for family and friends.

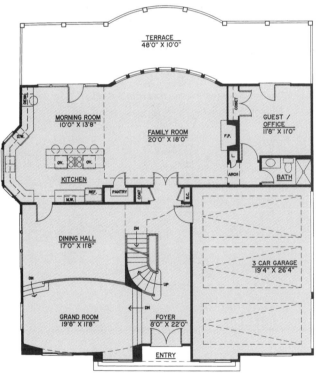

DESIGN HPT290002

©ARCHIVAL DESIGNS, INC.

DESIGN FEATURES

BEDROOMS: 4

BATHROOMS: 3½

FIRST FLOOR: 1,593 Sq. Ft.

SECOND FLOOR: 1,559 Sq. Ft.

TOTAL: 3,152 Sq. Ft.

WIDTH: 51'-0" DEPTH: 46'-6"

THIS HOME EXHIBITS SYMMETRY though the use of brick details, shutters and graceful columns. Inside, to the left of the two-story foyer and down a few steps is the slightly oval grand room. A spacious dining hall is just up three steps and offers direct access from the huge island kitchen. The family room, located at the rear of the home, features a bowed wall of windows and a warming fireplace. A guest room or office accesses to the rear deck as well as a full bath. Upstairs, the master suite is full of amenities, including two walk-in closets, a private porch and a lavish bath. Three family bedrooms, each with direct access to a bath, finish out this floor.

DESIGN HPT290003

©DESIGN BASICS, INC.

STEP BETWEEN THE COLUMNS and into the entry of this grand design. Large living and dining rooms flank a formal staircase. One of the most dramatic rooms in the house is the great room with a fourteen-foot beamed ceiling, a fireplace and wonderful views. Fancy the octagon-shaped breakfast nook or the kitchen with abundant counter space. This house incorporates four bedrooms, with the master bedroom on the first floor. A tiered ceiling, two walk-in closets and a luxurious bath with His and Hers vanities, a shower and a spa tub all characterize this suite. On the second floor, you'll find three bedrooms: two share a full bath and one has a private bath.

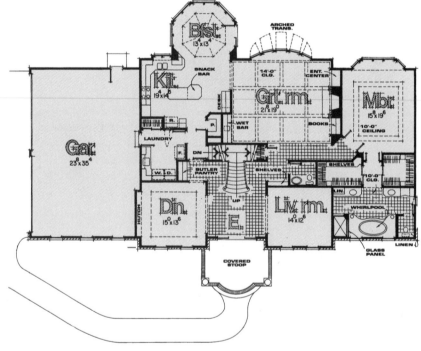

DESIGN FEATURES

BEDROOMS: 4

BATHROOMS: 3½

FIRST FLOOR: 2,500 Sq. Ft.

SECOND FLOOR: 973 Sq. Ft.

TOTAL: 3,473 Sq. Ft.

WIDTH: 84'-0" DEPTH: 52'-0"

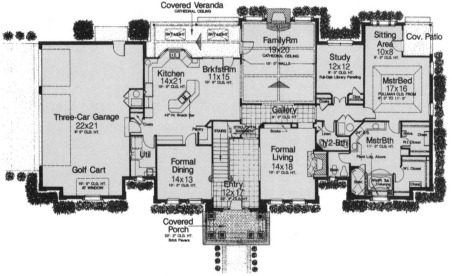

DESIGN HPT290004
©FILLMORE DESIGN GROUP

DESIGN FEATURES

BEDROOMS: 4

BATHROOMS: 3½

FIRST FLOOR: 2,814 Sq. Ft.

SECOND FLOOR: 979 Sq. Ft.

TOTAL: 3,793 Sq. Ft.

WIDTH: 98'-0" DEPTH: 45'-10"

A COVERED, COLUMNED PORCH and symmetrically placed windows welcome you to this elegant brick home. The formal living room offers built-in bookshelves and one of two fireplaces; the other is in the spacious family room. A gallery running between these rooms leads to the sumptuous master suite, which includes a sitting area, a private covered patio and a bath with two walk-in closets, dual vanities, a large shower and garden tub. The step-saving kitchen features a work island and snack bar. The breakfast and family rooms have doors to the large covered veranda. Upstairs, you'll find three bedrooms and attic storage space. The three-car garage even has room for a golf cart.

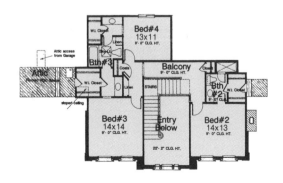

© American Home Gallery, Ltd.

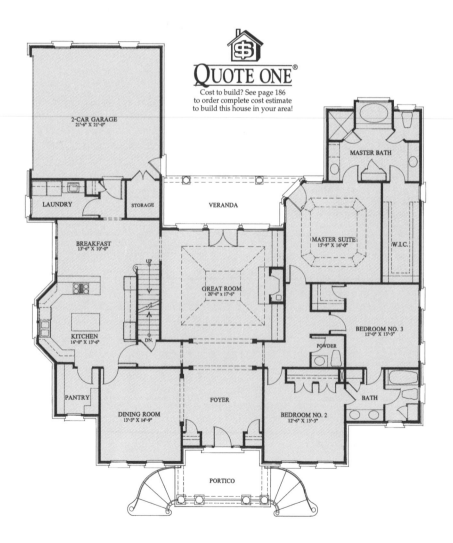

QUOTE ONE®
Cost to build? See page 186
to order complete cost estimate
to build this house in your area!

DESIGN HPT290005
©STEPHEN FULLER, INC.

DUAL CHIMNEYS (one a false chimney created to enhance the aesthetic effect) and a double stairway to the covered entry of this home create a balanced architectural statement. The sunlit foyer leads straight into the spacious great room, where French doors provide a generous view of the covered veranda in back. The great room features a tray ceiling and a fireplace, bordered by twin bookcases. Another great view is offered from the spacious kitchen with a breakfast bar and a roomy work island. The master suite provides a large balanced bath and a spacious closet. This home is designed with a walkout basement foundation.

DESIGN FEATURES
BEDROOMS: 3
BATHROOMS: 2½
TOTAL: 2,697 Sq. Ft.
WIDTH: 65'-3" DEPTH: 67'-3"

DESIGN HPT290006
©STEPHEN FULLER, INC.

THE GRACEFUL LINES of this formal Georgian brick manor are an inviting presence in any neighborhood. An open foyer enjoys views of the back property through the living room, which features a fireplace framed with built-in bookshelves. Dinner guests will want to linger on the rear terrace, which opens through French doors from formal and casual areas. The gourmet kitchen has a cook-top island, a walk-in pantry and a breakfast area that's open to the bright family room. Homeowners will enjoy the master bedroom's private sitting area, which features two skylights, a fireplace and access to the terrace. This home is designed with a walkout basement foundation.

DESIGN FEATURES

BEDROOMS: 4
BATHROOMS: 3½
FIRST FLOOR: 3,365 Sq. Ft.
SECOND FLOOR: 1,456 Sq. Ft.
TOTAL: 4,821 Sq. Ft.
BONUS ROOM: 341 Sq. Ft.
WIDTH: 81'-0"   DEPTH: 71'-9"

DESIGN HPT290007

©STEPHEN FULLER, INC.

DESIGN FEATURES

BEDROOMS: 4

BATHROOMS: 3½

FIRST FLOOR: 1,455 Sq. Ft.

SECOND FLOOR: 1,649 Sq. Ft.

TOTAL: 3,104 Sq. Ft.

WIDTH: 53'-0"   DEPTH: 46'-0"

THE DOUBLE WINGS, twin chimneys and center portico of this home work in concert to create a classic architectural statement. The two-story foyer is flanked by the spacious dining room and the formal living room, each containing its own fireplace. A large family room with a full wall of glass beckons the outside in and opens conveniently to the sunlit kitchen and breakfast room. The master suite features a tray ceiling and French doors that open to a covered porch. A grand bath with all the amenities, including a garden tub and huge walk-in closet, completes the master suite. The fourth bedroom also features a sunny nook for sitting or reading. This home is designed with a walkout basement foundation.

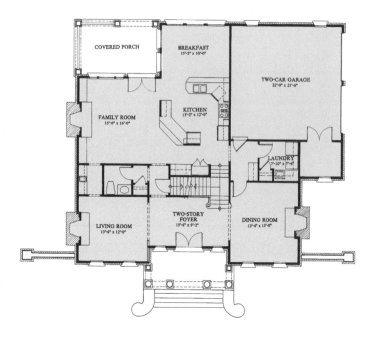

DESIGN HPT290008

©BRELAND & FARMER
DESIGNERS, INC.

NINE-FOOT CEILINGS

and shady upper and lower porticos make this a perfect retreat for long, hot summers. The living room is cozy year-round with built-ins, a fireplace and a raised tray ceiling. The first-floor master suite has its own porch retreat and a pampering bath with His and Hers vanities, walk-in closets, compartmented toilet and separate tub and shower. Three family bedrooms share a full bath on the second floor. A storage room in the garage prevents climbing up to the hot attic. Please specify basement, crawlspace or slab foundation when ordering.

DESIGN FEATURES

BEDROOMS: 4
BATHROOMS: 2½
FIRST FLOOR: 1,750 Sq. Ft.
SECOND FLOOR: 855 Sq. Ft.
TOTAL: 2,605 Sq. Ft.
WIDTH: 77'-0" DEPTH: 58'-0"

W.I.C.

MASTER SUITE
16'-0" X 13'-3"

SITTING
12'-0" X 13'-3"

BEDROOM NO. 2
13'-6" X 11'-6"

BATH

MASTER BATH

BEDROOM NO. 3
13'-9" X 12'-0"

BATH

W.I.C.

BEDROOM NO. 4
13'-0" X 12'-3"

DN.

OPEN TO BELOW

HIS **HERS**

UNFIN. STORAGE
10'-6" X 11'-6"

DESIGN FEATURES

BEDROOMS: 4

BATHROOMS: 3½

FIRST FLOOR: 1,554 Sq. Ft.

SECOND FLOOR: 1,648 Sq. Ft.

TOTAL: 3,202 Sq. Ft.

BONUS ROOM: 132 Sq. Ft.

WIDTH: 60'-0" DEPTH: 43'-0"

DESIGN HPT290009
©STEPHEN FULLER, INC.

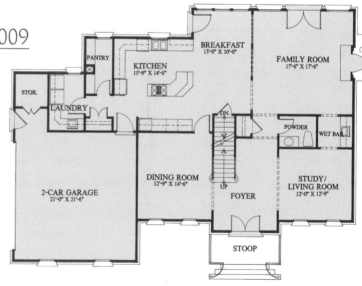

PANTRY

BREAKFAST
13'-0" X 10'-0"

KITCHEN
15'-9" X 14'-6"

FAMILY ROOM
17'-6" X 17'-6"

STOR.

LAUNDRY

DN.

POWDER

WET BAR

2-CAR GARAGE
21'-0" X 21'-6"

DINING ROOM
12'-9" X 14'-6"

UP

FOYER

STUDY/ LIVING ROOM
12'-0" X 12'-9"

STOOP

THE CLASSIC STYLING of this brick American traditional home will be respected for years to come. The formidable, double-door, transomed entry and a Palladian window reveal the shining foyer within, which is flanked by the spacious dining room and the formal study or living room. A large family room with a full wall of glass conveniently opens to the breakfast room and kitchen. The master suite features a spacious sitting area with its own fireplace and tray ceiling. Two additional bedrooms share a bath, while a fourth bedroom has its own private bath. This home is designed with a walkout basement foundation.

DESIGN HPT290010

©STEPHEN FULLER, INC.

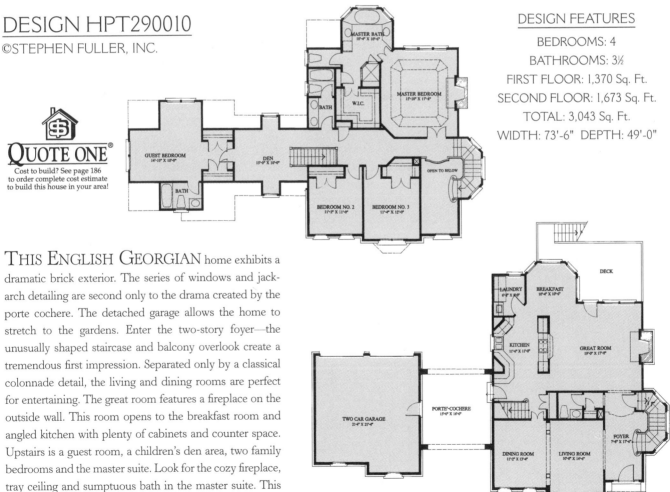

DESIGN FEATURES

BEDROOMS: 4
BATHROOMS: 3½
FIRST FLOOR: 1,370 Sq. Ft.
SECOND FLOOR: 1,673 Sq. Ft.
TOTAL: 3,043 Sq. Ft.
WIDTH: 73'-6" DEPTH: 49'-0"

THIS ENGLISH GEORGIAN home exhibits a dramatic brick exterior. The series of windows and jack-arch detailing are second only to the drama created by the porte cochere. The detached garage allows the home to stretch to the gardens. Enter the two-story foyer—the unusually shaped staircase and balcony overlook create a tremendous first impression. Separated only by a classical colonnade detail, the living and dining rooms are perfect for entertaining. The great room features a fireplace on the outside wall. This room opens to the breakfast room and angled kitchen with plenty of cabinets and counter space. Upstairs is a guest room, a children's den area, two family bedrooms and the master suite. Look for the cozy fireplace, tray ceiling and sumptuous bath in the master suite. This home is designed with a walkout basement foundation.

THE ENTRY TO THIS CLASSIC HOME is framed with a sweeping double staircase and four large columns topped with a pediment. The two-story foyer is flanked by spacious living and dining rooms. Beyond the foyer, the home is designed with rooms that offer maximum livability. The two-story family room, which has a central fireplace, opens to the study and a solarium. A spacious U-shaped kitchen features a central island cooktop. An additional staircase off the breakfast room offers convenient access to the second floor. The impressive master suite features backyard access and a bath fit for royalty. A walk-in closet with an ironing board will provide room for everything. Four bedrooms upstairs enjoy large proportions. This home is designed with a walkout basement foundation.

DESIGN HPT290011

©STEPHEN FULLER, INC.

DESIGN FEATURES

BEDROOMS: 5

BATHROOMS: 3½

FIRST FLOOR: 3,902 Sq. Ft.

SECOND FLOOR: 2,159 Sq. Ft.

TOTAL: 6,061 Sq. Ft.

WIDTH: 85'-3" DEPTH: 74'-0"

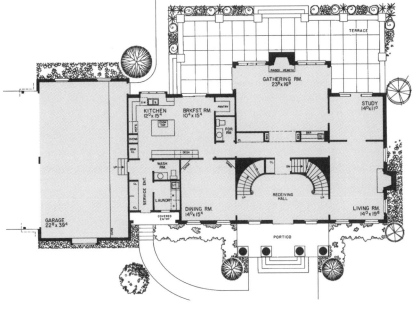

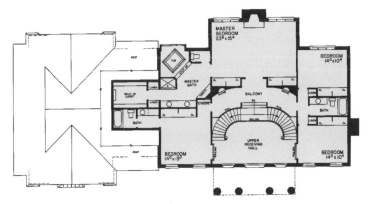

DESIGN HPT290012
©HOME PLANNERS

THIS CLASSIC GEORGIAN design contains a variety of features that make it outstanding: a pediment gable with cornice work and dentils, beautifully proportioned columns and distinct window treatment. The first floor contains some special appointments, including a fireplace in the living room and another fireplace and a wet bar in the gathering room. Upstairs, an extension over the garage allows for a huge walk-in closet in the master suite and a full bath in one of the family bedrooms.

DESIGN FEATURES

BEDROOMS: 4

BATHROOMS: 3½ + ½

FIRST FLOOR: 2,348 Sq. Ft.

SECOND FLOOR: 1,872 Sq. Ft.

TOTAL: 4,220 Sq. Ft.

WIDTH: 90'-4" DEPTH: 44'-8"

DESIGN HPT290013

©DESIGN BASICS, INC.

STATELY COLUMNS HIGHLIGHT the facade of this beautiful Southern Colonial home. The open entry allows for views into formal areas and up the tapering staircase. The dining room joins the kitchen through double doors. The living room can be divided from the sunken family room by pocket doors. Step down into the huge family room to find large windows, a fireplace, a built-in entertainment center and bookcases. The kitchen features a gazebo breakfast area, serving bar and cooktop island. Upstairs, three family bedrooms share two full baths. The private master suite features a tiered ceiling, two walk-in closets and a roomy, bayed sitting area.

DESIGN FEATURES

BEDROOMS: 4

BATHROOMS: 3½

FIRST FLOOR: 1,717 Sq. Ft.

SECOND FLOOR: 1,518 Sq. Ft.

TOTAL: 3,235 Sq. Ft.

WIDTH: 78'-0" DEPTH: 42'-0"

Quote One®

Cost to build? See page 186
to order complete cost estimate
to build this house in your area!

MAIN- AND SECOND-LEVEL COVERED PORCHES, accompanied by intricate detailing and many multi-pane windows, create a splendid Southern mansion. The prominent entry opens to formal dining and living rooms. The grand family room is warmed by a fireplace and views a screened porch with a cozy window seat. The roomy breakfast area provides access to the porch and the three-car garage. French doors open to the second floor's master suite, which features decorative ceiling details, His and Hers walk-in closets, a large dressing area, dual lavs, a whirlpool bath and a separate shower area. Three family bedrooms all offer direct bath access, completing the second floor.

DESIGN HPT290014
©DESIGN BASICS, INC.

DESIGN FEATURES

BEDROOMS: 4
BATHROOMS: 3½
FIRST FLOOR: 1,598 Sq. Ft.
SECOND FLOOR: 1,675 Sq. Ft.
TOTAL: 3,273 Sq. Ft.
BONUS ROOM: 534 Sq. Ft.
WIDTH: 54'-8" DEPTH: 68'-0"

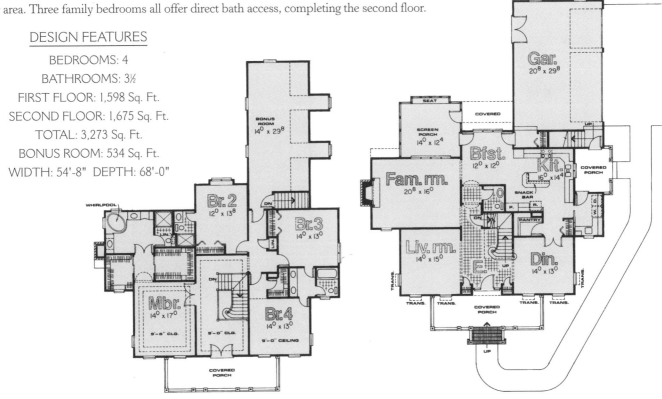

DESIGN HPT290015

©ARCHIVAL DESIGNS, INC.

DESIGN FEATURES

BEDROOMS: 3

BATHROOMS: 3

FIRST FLOOR: 1,815 Sq. Ft.

SECOND FLOOR: 699 Sq. Ft.

TOTAL: 2,514 Sq. Ft.

WIDTH: 55'-0" DEPTH: 49'-6"

A VISIT TO GREEK REVIVAL ARCHITECTURE brings you this beautiful three-bedroom home. Through four Romanesque columns you enter the foyer, which is flanked by a library to the left and a formal dining room to the right. Ahead is the spacious living room, complete with a fireplace. The U-shaped kitchen offers an adjacent breakfast room, as well as plenty of counter space. A guest suite/study opens off this area, and presents a full bath for privacy. Located on the main floor, the lavish master suite is designed to pamper, with a huge walk-in closet, sumptuous bath and a bayed wall. Note the private entrance to the library. Upstairs, two bedrooms, each with walk-in closets, share a full bath. An optional playroom is at the other end of the hall.

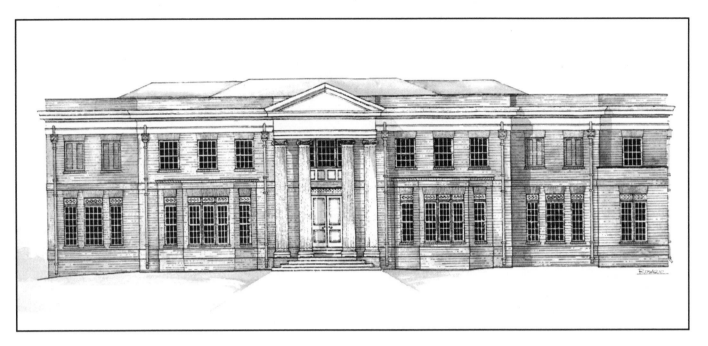

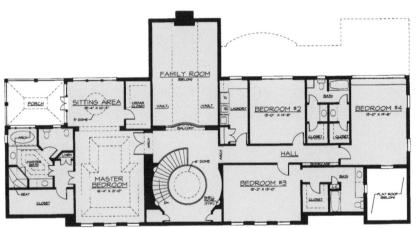

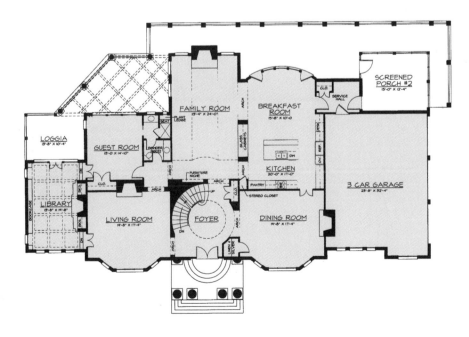

DESIGN HPT290016
©ARCHIVAL DESIGNS, INC.

YOU'VE PROBABLY SEEN homes like this—on BBC or PBS specials. They're usually inhabited by landed gentry who've inherited the structure from generations of ancestors. But this rendition is thoroughly modern and completely yours to decorate and enjoy. And you won't find any cramped, drafty areas inside—the floor plan is spacious and flexible enough for formal dinners and raucous Superbowl parties. Note the guest suite on the first floor near the library (a loggia access enhances the beamed-ceiling library). The family room is huge, and close enough to the breakfast room and kitchen to make it practical. A screened porch is a bonus. The grand staircase separates the master suite on the second floor from secondary bedrooms. A large cedar closet, sitting area and private porch reinforce the luxury here.

DESIGN FEATURES

BEDROOMS: 5
BATHROOMS: 4½
FIRST FLOOR: 2,538 Sq. Ft.
SECOND FLOOR: 2,491 Sq. Ft.
TOTAL: 5,029 Sq. Ft.
WIDTH: 94'-0" DEPTH: 48'-0"

23

THIS MAGNIFICENT BRICK FACADE is just a hint of the wonderful floor plan inside. The two-story foyer is flanked by the formal areas of the dining room and the living room—note the lack of cross-room traffic in both rooms. The efficient island kitchen offers plenty of counter and cabinet space and presents an octagonal breakfast room. A cathedral ceiling in the family room highlights the warming fireplace. Located on the first floor for privacy, the master suite is designed to pamper with a fireplace, built-in bookcases, a huge walk-in closet and a lavish bath. Upstairs, three family bedrooms share a full hall bath. Unfinished storage space is also available on this level for future development.

DESIGN HPT290017
©DESIGN BASICS, INC.

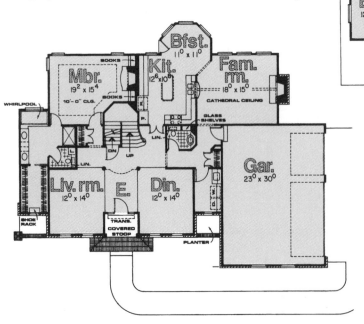

DESIGN FEATURES
BEDROOMS: 4
BATHROOMS: 2½
FIRST FLOOR: 1,878 Sq. Ft.
SECOND FLOOR: 719 Sq. Ft.
TOTAL: 2,597 Sq. Ft.
WIDTH: 68'-8" DEPTH: 52'-8"

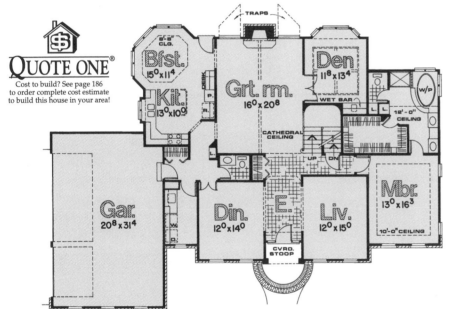

DESIGN HPT290018

©DESIGN BASICS, INC.

DESIGN FEATURES

BEDROOMS: 4

BATHROOMS: 4½

FIRST FLOOR: 2,063 Sq. Ft.

SECOND FLOOR: 894 Sq. Ft.

TOTAL: 2,957 Sq. Ft.

WIDTH: 72'-8" DEPTH: 51'-4"

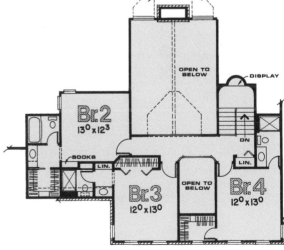

AN ELEGANT BRICK ELEVATION and rows of shuttered windows lend timeless beauty to this two-story Colonial design. The volume entry opens to the formal dining and living rooms and the magnificent great room. Sparkling floor-to-ceiling windows flank the fireplace in the great room, which offers a cathedral ceiling. French doors, bayed windows and a decorative ceiling, plus a wet bar highlight the private den. Special lifestyle amenities in the kitchen and bayed breakfast area include a built-in desk, wrapping counters and an island. A boxed ceiling adds elegance to the master suite. In the master bath/dressing area, note the large walk-in closet, His and Hers vanities, oval whirlpool tub and plant shelves. Each secondary bedroom upstairs has a roomy closet and private bath.

HISTORIC INDULGENCE

DESIGN FEATURES

BEDROOMS: 4

BATHROOMS: 3½

FIRST FLOOR: 2,920 Sq. Ft.

SECOND FLOOR: 853 Sq. Ft.

TOTAL: 3,773 Sq. Ft.

BONUS ROOM: 458 Sq. Ft.

WIDTH: 78'-7" DEPTH: 75'-7"

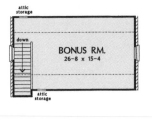

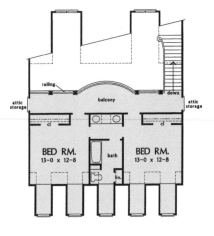

DESIGN HPT290019

DONALD A. GARDNER
ARCHITECTS, INC.

© 1996 Donald A. Gardner Architects, Inc.

THIS HOME HAS A TRADITIONAL symmetry in design that is a hallmark of Southern homes. The welcome feel of the front porch is translated throughout the plan with an open arrangement of the formal living and dining rooms and the expansive great room. The kitchen is designed for efficiency with a nearby laundry room and a large breakfast nook. The master bedroom contains an elegant tray ceiling and a posh bath. Upstairs, a balcony hall leads to two family bedrooms that share a compartmented bath.

DESIGN HPT290020
©STEPHEN FULLER, INC.

Quote One®
Cost to build? See page 186
to order complete cost estimate
to build this house in your area!

DESIGN FEATURES
BEDROOMS: 4
BATHROOMS: 3½
FIRST FLOOR: 1,960 Sq. Ft.
SECOND FLOOR: 905 Sq. Ft.
TOTAL: 2,865 Sq. Ft.
BONUS ROOM: 297 Sq. Ft.
WIDTH: 61'-0" DEPTH: 70'-6"

TRADITIONALISTS WILL APPRECIATE the classic styling of this
Colonial home. The foyer opens to both a banquet-sized dining room and the formal living room with a fireplace. Just beyond is the two-story great room. The entire
right side of the main level is taken up by the master suite. The other side of the main
level includes a large kitchen and breakfast room just steps away from the detached
garage. Upstairs, each bedroom features ample closet space and direct access to a
bath. The detached garage features an unfinished office or studio on its second level.
This home is designed with a walkout basement foundation.

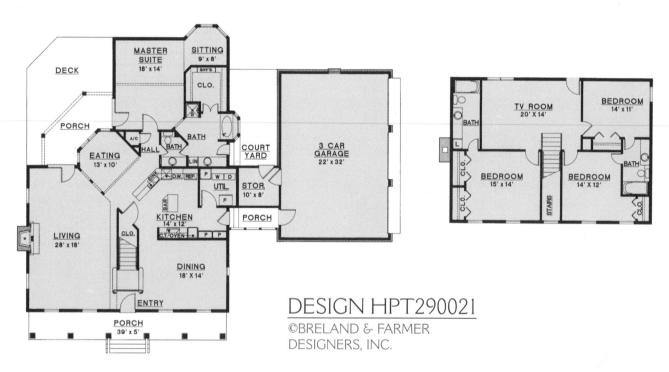

DESIGN HPT290021
©BRELAND & FARMER
DESIGNERS, INC.

DESIGN FEATURES

BEDROOMS: 4

BATHROOMS: 3½

FIRST FLOOR: 1,768 Sq. Ft.

SECOND FLOOR: 1,120 Sq. Ft.

TOTAL: 2,888 Sq. Ft.

WIDTH: 72'-0" DEPTH: 58'-0"

A SYMMETRICAL EXTERIOR with two-story columns adds grandeur to this home. The entry is flanked by the formal dining room and a living room that boasts a fireplace and a multitude of windows. A large angled kitchen is nestled between the dining room and the bayed eating area. The master suite enjoys a bayed sitting area and a pampering private bath. Three additional bedrooms and a TV room are found on the second floor. Three porches, a deck and a courtyard make for wonderful outdoor entertaining possibilities. Please specify basement, crawlspace or slab foundation when ordering.

DESIGN HPT290022

©BRELAND & FARMER
DESIGNERS, INC.

A PORCH WITH WOOD railings borders the facade of this plan, lending a farmhouse or country feel. The family room includes a fireplace and French doors to the porch, which opens further to the deck area. The master bedroom is filled with luxuries, from the walk-in closet with shelves, the full bath with a skylight, sloped ceiling and vanity, to the shower with a convenient seat. Three additional bedrooms upstairs share two full baths between them. A breezeway, placed between the garage and the house, leads easily to the deck area. Extras include a large utility room, pantry, half-bath downstairs and two storage areas. Please specify basement, crawlspace or slab foundation when ordering.

DESIGN FEATURES

BEDROOMS: 4
BATHROOMS: 3½
FIRST FLOOR: 2,008 Sq. Ft.
SECOND FLOOR: 1,027 Sq. Ft.
TOTAL: 3,035 Sq. Ft.
WIDTH: 66'-0" DEPTH: 74'-0"

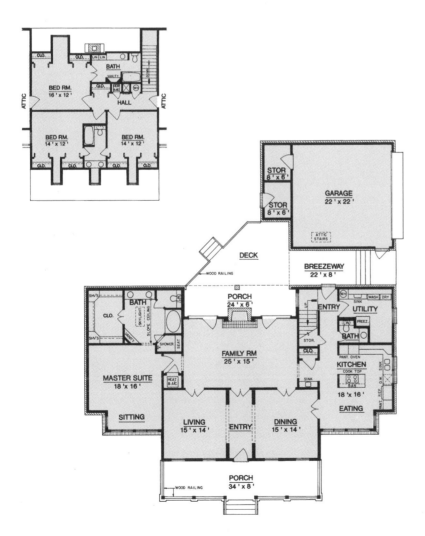

DESIGN FEATURES

BEDROOMS: 4
BATHROOMS: 3
TOTAL: 2,863 Sq. Ft.
BONUS SPACE: 987 Sq. Ft.
WIDTH: 73'-8" DEPTH: 97'-9"

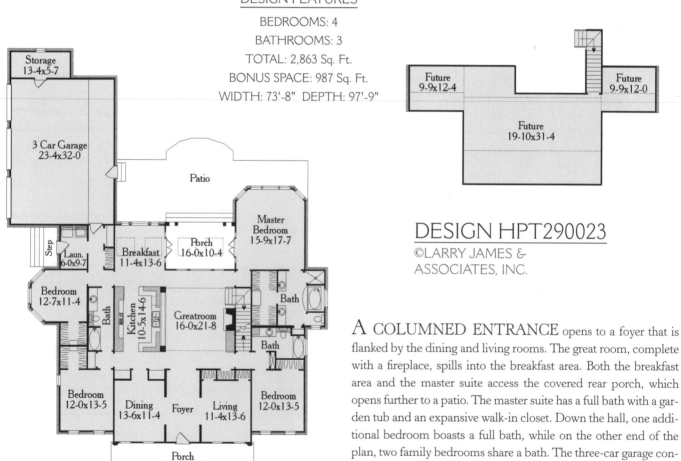

DESIGN HPT290023
©LARRY JAMES &
ASSOCIATES, INC.

A COLUMNED ENTRANCE opens to a foyer that is flanked by the dining and living rooms. The great room, complete with a fireplace, spills into the breakfast area. Both the breakfast area and the master suite access the covered rear porch, which opens further to a patio. The master suite has a full bath with a garden tub and an expansive walk-in closet. Down the hall, one additional bedroom boasts a full bath, while on the other end of the plan, two family bedrooms share a bath. The three-car garage contains attached storage space. Please specify basement, crawlspace or slab foundation when ordering.

DESIGN HPT290024

©LARRY JAMES & ASSOCIATES, INC.

COLUMNS, TRANSOM WINDOWS and
an eyebrow dormer lend this house a stylish country
charm. Inside, a built-in media center, a fireplace, skylights and columns add to the wonderful livability of this
home. Escape to the relaxing master suite, which features a private sitting room and a luxurious bath set
between His and Hers walk-in closets. Three bedrooms
share a bath on the other side of the plan, ensuring privacy. Please specify basement, crawlspace or slab foundation when ordering.

DESIGN FEATURES

BEDROOMS: 4

BATHROOMS: 2

TOTAL: 2,360 Sq. Ft.

WIDTH: 75'-2" DEPTH: 68'-0"

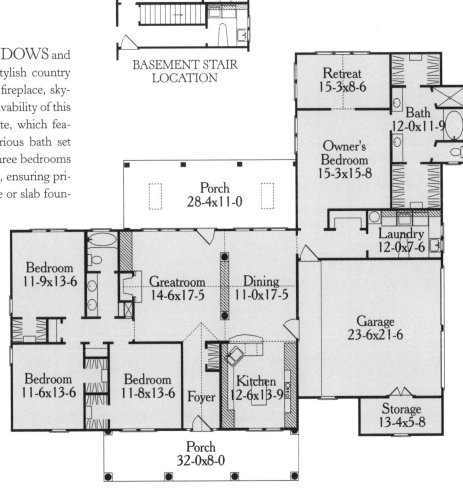

BASEMENT STAIR
LOCATION

C OLUMNS ON THE FRONT of this home mark it with grace and style and dress up its sunny stucco facade. Columns also grace the rear with another covered porch. The floor plan holds open living areas: a great room with a fireplace, a dining room, a U-shaped kitchen and a breakfast room. Columns are the defining point between the great room and the dining room. Family bedrooms on the right side of the plan are separated by a full bath. The master suite is tucked away behind the garage and contains a huge walk-in closet and a bath with a whirlpool tub. Note the extra storage space in the garage. Please specify crawlspace or slab foundation when ordering.

DESIGN HPT290025

©LARRY JAMES &
ASSOCIATES, INC.

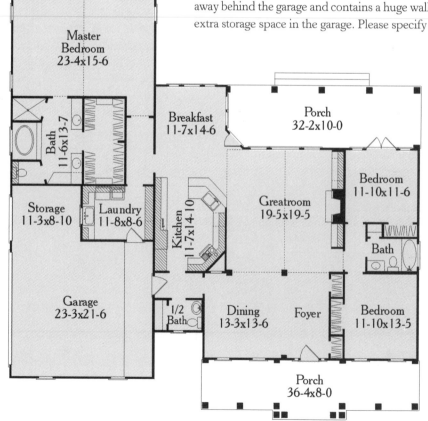

DESIGN FEATURES

BEDROOMS: 3
BATHROOMS: 2½
TOTAL: 2,424 Sq. Ft.
WIDTH: 68'-2" DEPTH: 67'-6"

EUROPEAN HOMES POSSESS A DISTINCTIVE FLAIR,

offering wonderful detailing and an Old World look. In general, French

and English homes feature exteriors of stone, brick and stucco, alone or

in combinations. Decorative stickwork is common, as are small-pane

windows and keystone arches, often with double rows of bricks or stones.

Roofs may be either hip or gable, with a variety of interesting planes and

angles and a wide use of dormers. Arched windows with decorative (yet

useful) drip stones are prevalent, as are grand entrances. Styles such as

the French farmhouse, English Tudor, Italian villa and the turreted

Norman (is it French or English?) are featured here, each full of ameni-

ties, grandeur and presence.

SHOWN ABOVE:

DESIGN HPT290033

BY FRANK BETZ

ASSOCIATES, INC.

SEE PAGE 41 FOR

MORE INFORMATION

ON THIS FINELY

DETAILED, FOUR-

BEDROOM HOME.

DESIGN HPT290026
©STEPHEN FULLER, INC.

THIS ENGLISH MANOR HOME features a dramatic brick-and-stucco exterior accented by a gabled roofline and artful half-timbering. Inside, the foyer opens to the formal living room accented with a vaulted ceiling and box-bay window. The dining room flows directly off the living room and features its own angled bay window. Through the double doors lies the center of family activity. An entire wall of glass, accented by a central fireplace, spans from the family room through to the breakfast area and kitchen. For your guests, a bedroom and bath are located on the main level. The second floor provides two additional bedrooms and a bath for children. The master suite—with its tray ceiling, fireplace and private study—is a pleasant retreat. This home is designed with a walkout basement foundation.

DESIGN FEATURES

BEDROOMS: 4

BATHROOMS: 3½

FIRST FLOOR: 1,678 Sq. Ft.

SECOND FLOOR: 1,677 Sq. Ft.

TOTAL: 3,355 Sq. Ft.

WIDTH: 50'-0" DEPTH: 50'-6"

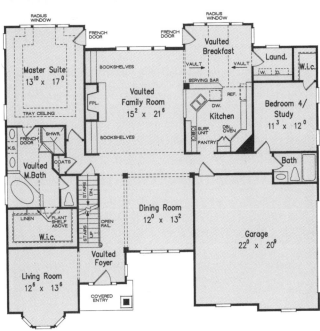

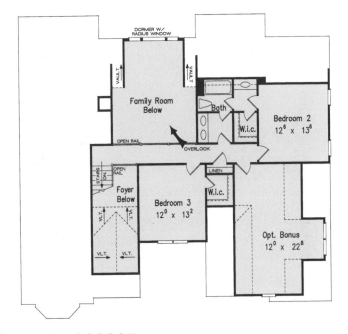

THE FORMAL LIVING ROOM opens directly off the vaulted foyer. An efficient kitchen serves the family room, vaulted breakfast room and the dining room. A secluded study can double as a guest suite, while the master suite enjoys privacy at the rear of the first floor. A full bath and two family bedrooms with walk-in closets are located on the second floor. The optional bonus room is available for future expansion. Please specify basement or crawl-space foundation when ordering.

DESIGN HPT290027

©FRANK BETZ
ASSOCIATES, INC.

DESIGN FEATURES

BEDROOMS: 4

BATHROOMS: 3

FIRST FLOOR: 2,015 Sq. Ft.

SECOND FLOOR: 628 Sq. Ft.

TOTAL: 2,643 Sq. Ft.

BONUS ROOM: 315 Sq. Ft.

WIDTH: 56'-0" DEPTH: 52'-6"

DESIGN HPT290028

©FRANK BETZ
ASSOCIATES, INC.

DESIGN FEATURES

BEDROOMS: 4

BATHROOMS: 3½

FIRST FLOOR: 2,467 Sq. Ft.

SECOND FLOOR: 928 Sq. Ft.

TOTAL: 3,395 Sq. Ft.

BONUS ROOM: 296 Sq. Ft.

WIDTH: 64'-6" DEPTH: 62'-10"

A CHIC COMBINATION OF EUROPEAN STYLE and farmhouse charm gives this two-story home an eclectic appeal. Apart from the private living room, living areas are open and divided by decorative columns at the dining room and the vaulted great room. The spacious kitchen has wraparound counters, a serving bar and a sunny breakfast room. The master suite contains a lovely, vaulted sitting room with a three-sided fireplace and a spa-style bath. Upstairs, two bedrooms share a bath, while another has a private bath. Please specify basement, crawlspace or slab foundation when ordering.

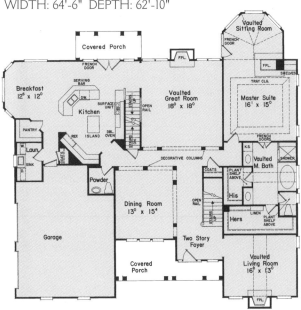

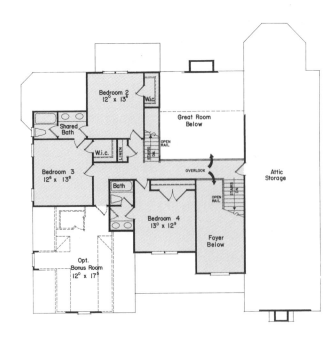

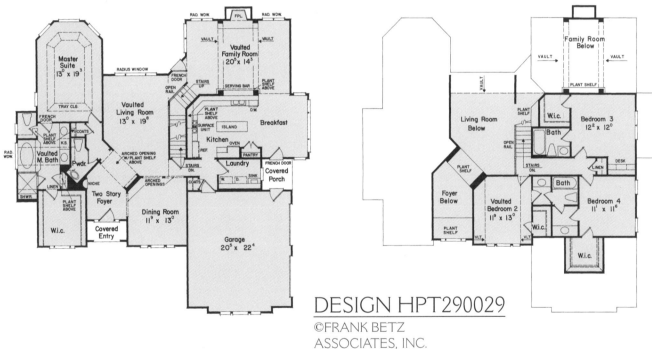

DESIGN HPT290029
©FRANK BETZ
ASSOCIATES, INC.

DESIGN FEATURES
BEDROOMS: 4
BATHROOMS: 3½
FIRST FLOOR: 1,883 Sq. Ft.
SECOND FLOOR: 803 Sq. Ft.
TOTAL: 2,686 Sq. Ft.
WIDTH: 58'-6" DEPTH: 59'-4"

A GRAND FACADE IS A PERFECT INTRODUCTION to this stately two-story home that's designed for both formal and casual family living. A two-story foyer that leads to the vaulted living room is punctuated by a dramatic arch with a plant shelf above. Formal entertaining areas are nicely balanced with the vaulted family room and the gourmet kitchen and breakfast nook. The first-floor master suite is designed for luxury and privacy. Upstairs, three family bedrooms each have a walk-in closet and private bath access. Please specify basement or crawlspace foundation when ordering.

DESIGN HPT290030

©FRANK BETZ
ASSOCIATES, INC.

DESIGN FEATURES

BEDROOMS: 4

BATHROOMS: 3½

FIRST FLOOR: 2,302 Sq. Ft.

SECOND FLOOR: 845 Sq. Ft.

TOTAL: 3,147 Sq. Ft.

BONUS ROOM: 247 Sq. Ft.

WIDTH: 64'-0" DEPTH: 59'-4"

THE ARCHED FRONT DOORWAY bids a warm welcome to this spacious home. The formal dining room opens to the right, its outline is punctuated by decorative columns. The family and keeping rooms each have a fireplace and a vaulted ceiling, while the large kitchen offers a work island and a serving bar to make mealtimes in the breakfast nook a cinch. On the left side of the plan are a gazebo-shaped formal living room and the elegant master suite with a bayed sitting area. Two staircases lead to three family bedrooms and the optional bonus room upstairs. Please specify basement or crawlspace foundation when ordering.

DESIGN HPT290031

©FRANK BETZ
ASSOCIATES, INC.

QUOTE ONE®
Cost to build? See page 186
to order complete cost estimate
to build this house in your area!

A GRACIOUS FRONT PORCH in the formal dining room and a
two-story entry set the tone for this elegant home. A front living room resides
to the front of the plan, thoughtfully separated from casual family areas that
radiate from the kitchen. The two-story family room is framed by a balcony
hall and accented with a fireplace and serving bar. The first-floor master suite
features a sitting area, lush bath and walk-in closet. Upstairs, two family bedrooms share a full bath while a third enjoys a private bath. Please specify basement or crawlspace foundation when ordering.

DESIGN FEATURES

BEDROOMS: 4
BATHROOMS: 3½
FIRST FLOOR: 2,044 Sq. Ft.
SECOND FLOOR: 896 Sq. Ft.
TOTAL: 2,940 Sq. Ft.
BONUS ROOM: 197 Sq. Ft.
WIDTH: 63'-0" DEPTH: 54'-0"

DESIGN HPT290032

©FRANK BETZ
ASSOCIATES, INC.

DESIGN FEATURES

BEDROOMS: 3

BATHROOMS: 2½

TOTAL: 2,491 Sq. Ft.

BONUS SPACE: 588 Sq. Ft.

WIDTH: 64'-0" DEPTH: 72'-4"

EUROPEAN DETAILS BRING CHARM and a bit of *joie de vivre* to this traditional home, and a thoughtful floor plan warms up to a myriad of lifestyles. Comfortable living space includes a vaulted family room with a centered fireplace, and complements the formal dining room, which offers a tray ceiling. A sizable gourmet kitchen offers a walk-in pantry and a center cooktop island counter, and overlooks the breakfast area, which opens to a secluded covered porch through a French door. The master suite provides a tray ceiling and a private sitting room, bright with windows and a warming hearth. Please specify basement or crawlspace foundation when ordering.

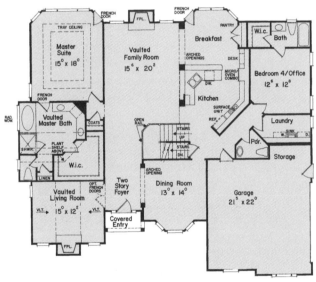

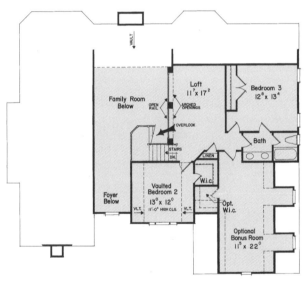

DESIGN HPT290033

©FRANK BETZ
ASSOCIATES, INC.

STUCCO, STONE AND INTRICATE DETAILING give this home a pleasing facade. Inside, the two-story foyer leads to a family room with a welcoming fireplace. The kitchen shares open space with a sunlit, bayed breakfast room that includes French-door access to the backyard. A luxurious master suite and a corner office complete the first floor. Upstairs, two bedrooms share a full bath, and a loft overlooks the family room. Please specify basement or crawlspace foundation when ordering.

DESIGN FEATURES

BEDROOMS: 4
BATHROOMS: 3½
FIRST FLOOR: 2,211 Sq. Ft.
SECOND FLOOR: 719 Sq. Ft.
TOTAL: 2,930 Sq. Ft.
BONUS ROOM: 331 Sq. Ft.
WIDTH: 61'-0" DEPTH: 53'-6"

DESIGN HPT290034

©STEPHEN FULLER, INC.

DESIGN FEATURES

BEDROOMS: 4

BATHROOMS: 3

FIRST FLOOR: 1,847 Sq. Ft.

SECOND FLOOR: 1,453 Sq. Ft.

TOTAL: 3,300 Sq. Ft.

WIDTH: 63'-3" DEPTH: 47'-0"

TO SUIT THOSE WHO FAVOR CLASSIC EUROPEAN styling, this English Manor home features a dramatic brick exterior which is further emphasized by the varied roofline and the finial atop the uppermost gable. The main level opens to a two-story foyer, with the formal rooms on the right. The living room contains a fireplace set in a bay window. The dining room is separated from the living room by a symmetrical column arrangement. The more casual family room is to the rear. For guests, a bedroom and bath are located on the main level. The second floor provides additional bedrooms and baths for family as well as a magnificent master suite. This home is designed with a basement foundation.

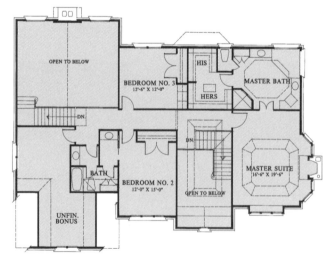

DESIGN HPT290035
©STEPHEN FULLER, INC.

DESIGN FEATURES

BEDROOMS: 5

BATHROOMS: 4

FIRST FLOOR: 1,683 Sq. Ft.

SECOND FLOOR: 1,544 Sq. Ft.

TOTAL: 3,227 Sq. Ft.

BONUS ROOM: 176 Sq. Ft.

WIDTH: 60'-0" DEPTH: 48'-6"

HANDSOMELY ARRANGED, this country cottage possesses an inviting quality. The stucco exterior, mixed with stone and shingles, creates a warmth that is accented with a fanlight transom and pendant door frame. The two-story foyer flows easily into the formal dining room and living room. The great room features a fireplace and bookcases on the side wall and opens to a well-lit breakfast and kitchen area. To complete the main level of this home, a guest room offers visitors the utmost in privacy. Provided upstairs are three additional bedrooms and a bonus space for an office or playroom. The master suite features a tray ceiling and an adjoining sitting area with special ceiling treatment. The private bath offers a large garden tub, separate vanities, His and Hers closets and an octagonal glass shower. This home is designed with a walkout basement foundation.

EUROPEAN LUXURY

DESIGN HPT290036

©STEPHEN FULLER, INC.

S<small>YMMETRY COMBINED WITH CLASSICAL</small> French detailing proclaims this estate as the very finest in elegant architecture. The double-door entry opens to an equally magnificent floor plan. Designed on the traditional center-hall principle, the home sustains both grand formal spaces and uniquely intimate casual areas. The study connects directly to the master suite, but also is accessed directly from the foyer—making it a fine home office. The living room is stately with built-ins, a raised hearth and outdoor access. For convenience, the master suite remains on the first floor. Elegant beyond compare, it spotlights a tray ceiling, His and Hers closets and a resplendent master bath. Family bedrooms are upstairs, along with a handy media room. This home is designed with a walkout basement foundation.

DESIGN FEATURES

BEDROOMS: 4
BATHROOMS: 3½
FIRST FLOOR: 2,923 Sq. Ft.
SECOND FLOOR: 1,689 Sq. Ft.
TOTAL: 4,612 Sq. Ft.
WIDTH: 75'-6" DEPTH: 58'-4"

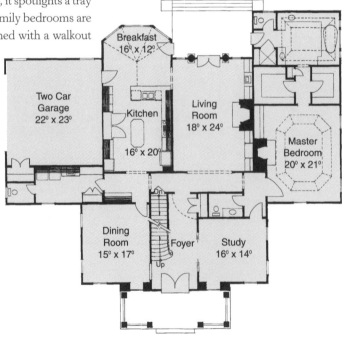

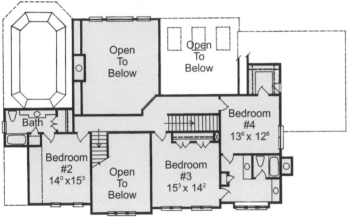

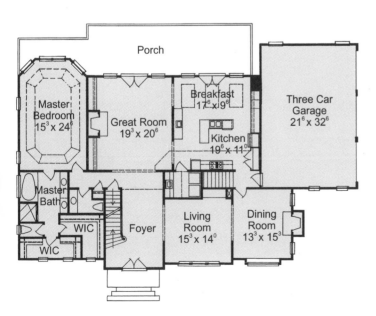

DESIGN HPT290037
©STEPHEN FULLER, INC.

MULTI-PANE GLASS WINDOWS, double French doors and ornamental stucco detailing are complementary elements on the facade of this home. An impressive two-story foyer opens to the formal living and dining rooms. Natural light is available through the attractive windows in each room. The kitchen features a pass-through to the two-story family room and an adjoining skylit breakfast room. The first-floor master suite offers an elegant vaulted bedroom ceiling, a bath with twin vanities, a separate shower and tub, and two spacious walk-in closets. Upstairs, Bedroom 2 has its own bath and can be used as a guest suite. Two other bedrooms share a large bath that includes twin vanities. This home is designed with a walkout basement foundation.

DESIGN FEATURES

BEDROOMS: 4
BATHROOMS: 3½
FIRST FLOOR: 2,420 Sq. Ft.
SECOND FLOOR: 1,146 Sq. Ft.
TOTAL: 3,566 Sq. Ft.
WIDTH: 77'-8" DEPTH: 50'-8"

EUROPEAN HOSPITALITY COMES TO MIND

with this home's high hipped roof, arched dormers and welcoming front porch. This clever and original two-story plan begins with the foyer opening to the staircase. At the end of the foyer, a spacious great room provides built-ins, a warming fireplace and double doors leading to the deck. The kitchen has excellent accommodations for preparation of meals, and the keeping room (with access to the deck) will make family gatherings comfortable. Note the storage space, powder room and pantry near the two-car garage. Inside the master suite, an enormous walk-in closet divides the bath, with its own shower, garden tub and double-bowl vanity. On the second floor, each bedroom has its own entrance to a full bath.

DESIGN HPT290038

©LIVING CONCEPTS
HOME PLANNING

DESIGN FEATURES

BEDROOMS: 4

BATHROOMS: 3½

FIRST FLOOR: 2,060 Sq. Ft.

SECOND FLOOR: 926 Sq. Ft.

TOTAL: 2,986 Sq. Ft.

WIDTH: 86'-0" DEPTH: 65'-5"

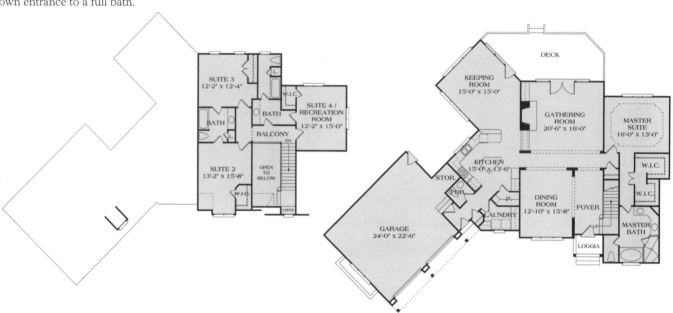

DESIGN FEATURES

BEDROOMS: 4

BATHROOMS: 4½

TOTAL: 3,960 Sq. Ft.

WIDTH: 96'-0" DEPTH: 90'-0"

DESIGN HPT290039

©BRELAND & FARMER
DESIGNERS, INC.

THIS HOME WILL MAKE a bold statement in any neighborhood. A one-of-a-kind design, this plan boasts varying levels of hipped rooflines, columns, shuttered windows and a large front arbor/porch. A foyer leads to the spacious family room, complete with a fireplace, while the dining room and living room flank the foyer. The kitchen area is comprised of an eating space, pantry and utility area—all of which are tiled. A large porch/deck area grace the rear of the house, and a sun room allows for plenty of lazy afternoons basking in the warmth. The decadent master suite boasts glass shelves and a sitting area with a fireplace, while additional shelves are found in the walk-in closet. Three additional bedrooms each have their own full bath. Two large storage areas positioned near the garage complete this plan. Please specify basement, crawlspace or slab foundation when ordering.

DESIGN HPT290040

©BRELAND & FARMER
DESIGNERS, INC.

COURTYARDS SET THE MOOD for this aged country cottage, beginning with the entry court. The narrow design of this three-bedroom plan makes it perfect for high-density areas where the homeowner still wants privacy. Sixteen-foot ceilings, a fireplace, an entertainment center and spacious views of the entry courtyard and dining room are all part of the amenities of the living room. The master suite has a fireplace and built-in entertainment center too! Please specify crawlspace or slab foundation when ordering.

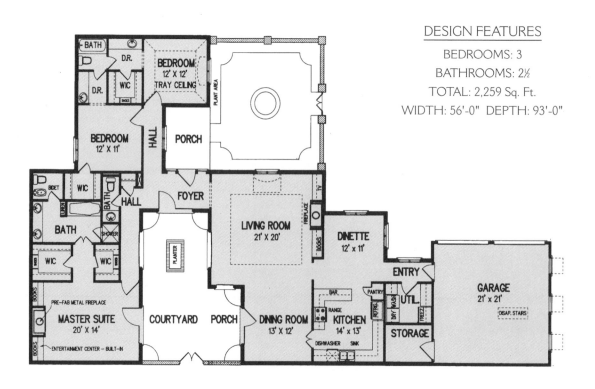

DESIGN FEATURES

BEDROOMS: 3
BATHROOMS: 2½
TOTAL: 2,259 Sq. Ft.
WIDTH: 56'-0" DEPTH: 93'-0"

A STONE-ACCENTED ENTRANCE welcomes you to this impressive French country estate. A sunken grand room combines with a bay-windowed dining room to create the formal living area. French doors open to a multi-level terrace that links formal and informal areas and the master suite. A screened porch off the gathering room has a pass-through window from the kitchen to facilitate warm-weather dining. The master wing on the right side of this design includes a study with a fireplace as well as a bayed sitting area and an amenity-laden bath. Two of the four bedrooms have private baths, while the others have separate dressing and vanity areas upstairs within a shared bath. A recreation room with a corner bar completes the plan.

DESIGN HPT290041
©LIVING CONCEPTS
HOME PLANNING

DESIGN FEATURES

BEDROOMS: 5

BATHROOMS: 4½ + ½

FIRST FLOOR: 3,387 Sq. Ft.

SECOND FLOOR: 1,799 Sq. Ft.

TOTAL: 5,186 Sq. Ft.

BONUS ROOM: 379 Sq. Ft.

WIDTH: 110'-10" DEPTH: 84'-6"

DESIGN FEATURES

BEDROOMS: 4
BATHROOMS: 3½ + ½
FIRST FLOOR: 3,172 Sq. Ft.
SECOND FLOOR: 1,238 Sq. Ft.
TOTAL: 4,410 Sq. Ft.
WIDTH: 86'-9" DEPTH: 85'-0"

A STUNNING EUROPEAN TRADITIONAL, this home is designed for the corner or pie-shaped lot. A three-way fireplace serves the kitchen, breakfast room and gathering room. The master suite and study are located in one wing. The private bath includes a whirlpool tub and a double shower. Three bedrooms, two baths and a game room are located upstairs. Please specify slab or crawlspace foundation when ordering.

DESIGN HPT290042
©LARRY E. BELK DESIGNS

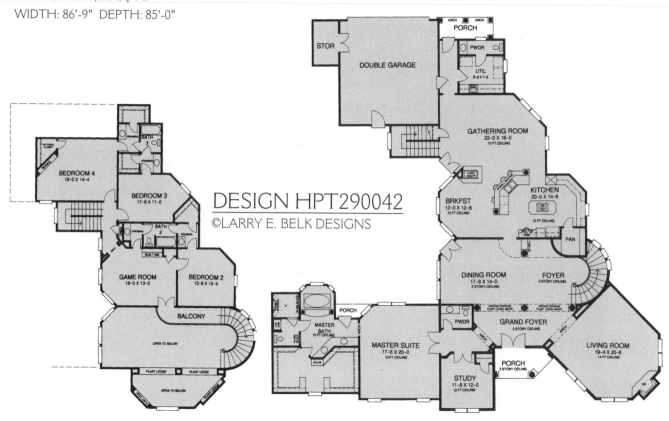

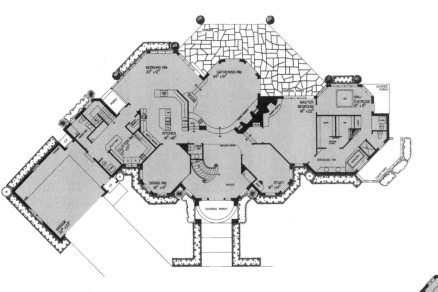

DESIGN FEATURES

BEDROOMS: 5
BATHROOMS: 5½ + ½
FIRST FLOOR: 3,736 Sq. Ft.
SECOND FLOOR: 2,264 Sq. Ft.
TOTAL: 6,000 Sq. Ft.
WIDTH: 133'-4" DEPTH: 65'-5"

L

THE DISTINCTIVE COVERED ENTRY to this stunning manor, flanked by twin turrets, leads to a gracious foyer with impressive fanlights. The plan opens from the foyer to a formal dining room, a study and a step-down gathering room. The spacious kitchen has numerous amenities, including an island work station and a built-in desk. The adjacent morning room and the gathering room, with a wet bar and a raised-hearth fireplace, are bathed in light and open to the terrace for outdoor entertaining. The luxurious and secluded master suite includes two walk-in closets, a dressing area and an exercise area with a spa. The second floor features four bedrooms and an oversized activities room with a fireplace and a balcony. Unfinished attic space can be completed to your specifications.

DESIGN HPT290043
©HOME PLANNERS

THIS COTTAGE-STYLE HOME looks as if it was nestled in the French countryside. The combination of brick, stone and rough cedar, and multiple chimneys add to the charm of the facade. The gracious two-story entry leads to all areas of the home. A beautiful, curving staircase leads to an upper balcony overlooking the entry. The second floor consists of three bedrooms, each with a connecting bath and walk-in closet. Space for a future playroom is located above the garage. Downstairs, the family area with a cathedral ceiling is open to the large kitchen and breakfast area. A large pantry is located near the kitchen. The cozy study has its own marble fireplace and a vaulted ceiling.

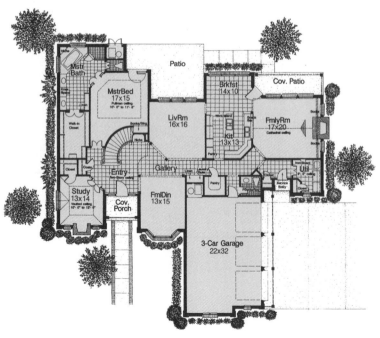

DESIGN HPT290044

©FILLMORE DESIGN GROUP

DESIGN FEATURES

BEDROOMS: 4

BATHROOMS: 3½

FIRST FLOOR: 2,700 Sq. Ft.

SECOND FLOOR: 990 Sq. Ft.

TOTAL: 3,690 Sq. Ft.

BONUS ROOM: 365 Sq. Ft.

WIDTH: 76'-0" DEPTH: 74'-1"

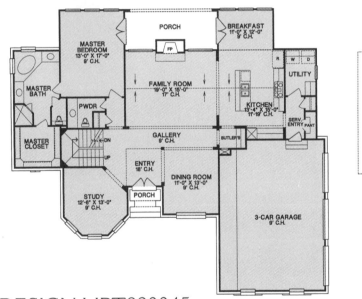

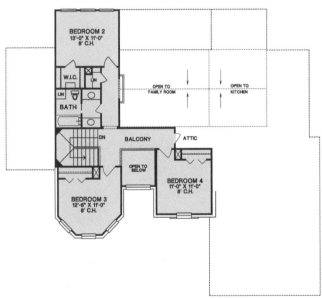

DESIGN HPT290045

©DESIGN BASICS, INC.

A HIPPED ROOF, BRICK EXTERIOR, TURRET, and keystones above the windows carry on the Old World legacy of European style. A soaring, two-story entry opens to a formal dining room on the right and an octagon-shaped study on the left. Beyond the gallery is a family room with a fireplace and views of the rear grounds. The nearby kitchen features an island work center, a sunny breakfast room that provides access to the rear porch and a butler's pantry that facilitates formal entertaining. Enjoying separate access to the rear porch, the master suite provides a relaxing, private retreat. A wall of windows naturally illuminates the master bedroom while the master bath offers the ultimate in luxury. The second floor contains three family bedrooms and a full bath. Please specify basement, block or slab foundation when ordering.

DESIGN FEATURES

BEDROOMS: 4
BATHROOMS: 2½
FIRST FLOOR: 1,906 Sq. Ft.
SECOND FLOOR: 749 Sq. Ft.
TOTAL: 2,655 Sq. Ft.
WIDTH: 65'-3"   DEPTH: 57'-2"

DESIGN HPT290046
©FILLMORE DESIGN GROUP

HERE A VOLUME ROOFLINE helps make the difference, both inside and out, allowing for vaulted ceilings in many of the interior spaces. There are more than enough living areas in this plan: formal living and dining rooms, a huge family room with a fireplace and a study with a bay window. The kitchen has an attached, light-filled breakfast area and is open to the family room. Four bedrooms include three family bedrooms; two on the right side of the plan and one on the left. The master suite features a private covered patio, a vaulted ceiling, two walk-in closets and a bath fit for a king. A three-car garage contains ample space for cars and recreational vehicles.

DESIGN FEATURES

BEDROOMS: 4
BATHROOMS: 3½
TOTAL: 3,056 Sq. Ft.
WIDTH: 80'-0" DEPTH: 79'-0"

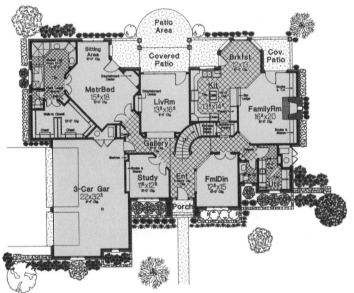

DESIGN HPT290047

©FILLMORE DESIGN GROUP

DESIGN FEATURES

BEDROOMS: 4

BATHROOMS: 3½

FIRST FLOOR: 2,496 Sq. Ft.

SECOND FLOOR: 1,090 Sq. Ft.

TOTAL: 3,586 Sq. Ft.

BONUS ROOM: 265 Sq. Ft.

WIDTH: 76'-0" DEPTH: 60'-0"

SOARING STONE AND BRICK GABLES combine to grace the exterior of this French country home, enhancing its European appeal. Inside, the two-story entry opens to a columned dining room on the right, through double doors to a study on the left, and straight ahead—an elegant, curving staircase and a gracious living room. The uniquely designed master suite contains a large walk-in closet and a luxurious master bath filled with amenities. An open floor plan brings the casual living areas together, connecting the island kitchen, octagonal breakfast room and family room. Passage to the rear covered patio is supplied by the breakfast room as well as the family room. The second floor is comprised of three family bedrooms—one with its own bath—and a full bath with separate dressing areas.

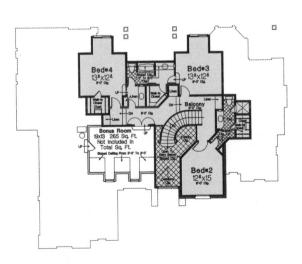

DESIGN HPT290048
©HOME DESIGN SERVICES, INC.

IMAGINE YOURSELF in the south of France with this French Provincial home. Inside, head straight for the beam-ceiling living room, which looks out to the covered porch. The breakfast room, kitchen and family room are all connected by the kitchen's island/snack bar. Enjoy formal dining at the front of the house, with a tray ceiling overhead. The master suite features a wall of windows, two walk-in closets and a luxurious private bath. Three bedrooms occupy the second level; two share a full bath, while the third includes a private bath. Other amenities include a den—which has a walk-in closet and French doors leading to a private garden—a wine cellar and a powder room off the garage for swimming parties.

DESIGN FEATURES

BEDROOMS: 4

BATHROOMS: 3½

FIRST FLOOR: 3,079 Sq. Ft.

SECOND FLOOR: 1,015 Sq. Ft.

TOTAL: 4,094 Sq. Ft.

BONUS ROOM: 425 Sq. Ft.

WIDTH: 77'-4" DEPTH: 82'-8"

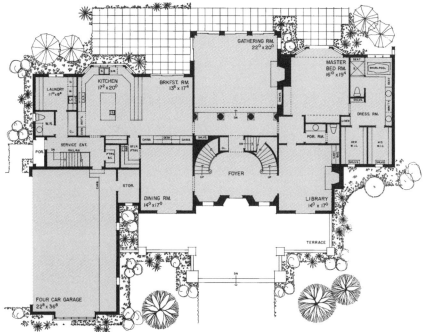

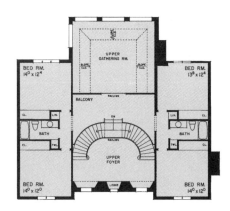

DESIGN HPT290049
©HOME PLANNERS

REMINISCENT OF A MEDITERRANEAN VILLA, this grand manor is a showstopper on the outside and a comfortable residence on the inside. An elegant receiving hall boasts a double staircase and is flanked by the formal dining room and the library. A huge gathering room to the back is graced by a fireplace and a wall of sliding glass doors to the rear terrace. The master bedroom is found on the first floor for privacy. With a lavish bath to pamper you, and His and Hers walk-in closets, this suite will be a delight to retire to each evening. Upstairs, four additional bedrooms with ample storage space, a large balcony overlooking the gathering room and two full baths complete the home.

DESIGN FEATURES
BEDROOMS: 5
BATHROOMS: 3½ + ½
FIRST FLOOR: 3,350 Sq. Ft.
SECOND FLOOR: 1,298 Sq. Ft.
TOTAL: 4,648 Sq. Ft.
WIDTH: 97'-0" DEPTH: 74'-4"

Photo courtesy of Living Concepts Home Planning

DESIGN HPT290050
©LIVING CONCEPTS HOME PLANNING

THIS ATTRACTIVE DESIGN is characterized by a wonderful symmetry and highlighted by a massive entry and cast-stone trim. Placing the garage in back, connected by a breezeway, makes the house adaptable to a narrow, deep lot. Entertaining will be easy, thanks to the centrally located grand room (with a fireplace), the nearby dining room and wet bar, and triple French doors to the terrace. Extra-large gatherings can spill over into the family room, with its own fireplace and access to a screened porch. A hobby room is found just off the kitchen. The homeowners will love the sumptuous first-floor master suite, but may be envious of the home theater and recreation room found on the second floor. Three more bedrooms with private baths complete this area, while bonus space over the garage awaits future development.

DESIGN FEATURES

BEDROOMS: 5
BATHROOMS: 5½ + ½
FIRST FLOOR: 3,129 Sq. Ft.
SECOND FLOOR: 2,298 Sq. Ft.
TOTAL: 5,427 Sq. Ft.
APARTMENT: 727 Sq. Ft.
WIDTH: 85'-0" DEPTH: 130'-0"

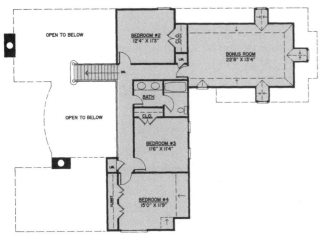

DESIGN HPT290051
©ARCHIVAL DESIGNS, INC.

THE GRACEFUL SWEEP of the facade, softened by molding details, sets this home apart from the crowd. Beneath the striking roofline is nestled a columned porch entry with double doors. The floor plan is equally impressive, highlighted by a dramatic bow-windowed, two-story great room with built-in shelves flanking the fireplace. At the right of the plan, the kitchen provides ample counter space plus an island. The adjacent breakfast room features an eighteen-foot ceiling and flows into the two-story keeping room with a second fireplace, vaulted ceiling and double doors to the deck. The master bedroom also opens to the deck through double doors and is accented by a tray ceiling and a bath with His and Hers closets, a dual vanity, oversized tub and separate shower. On the second floor, three additional bedrooms are joined by a balcony overlooking the great room, while a bonus room is available for future development.

DESIGN FEATURES

BEDROOMS: 4

BATHROOMS: 2½

FIRST FLOOR: 1,743 Sq. Ft.

SECOND FLOOR: 762 Sq. Ft.

TOTAL: 2,505 Sq. Ft.

BONUS ROOM: 361 Sq. Ft.

WIDTH: 47'-0" DEPTH: 68'-0"

DESIGN HPT290052
©STEPHEN FULLER, INC.

QUAINT, YET AS MAJESTIC as a country manor on the Rhine, this European-style stucco home enjoys the enchantment of arched windows to underscore its charm. The two-story foyer leads through French doors to the study with its own hearth and coffered ceiling. Coupled with this cozy sanctuary is the master suite with tray ceiling and large accommodating bath. The large, sunken great room is highlighted by a fireplace, built-in bookcases, lots of glass and easy access to a back stair and large gourmet kitchen. Three secondary bedrooms reside upstairs. One spacious upstairs bedroom gives guests the ultimate in convenience with a private bath and walk-in closet. This home is designed with a walkout basement foundation.

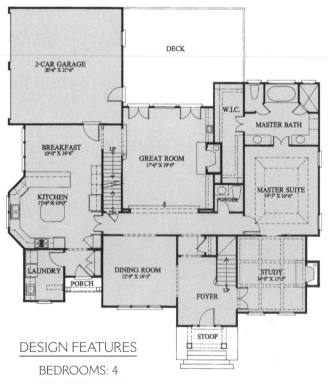

DESIGN FEATURES

BEDROOMS: 4

BATHROOMS: 3½

FIRST FLOOR: 2,208 Sq. Ft.

SECOND FLOOR: 1,250 Sq. Ft.

TOTAL: 3,458 Sq. Ft.

WIDTH: 60'-6" DEPTH: 60'-0"

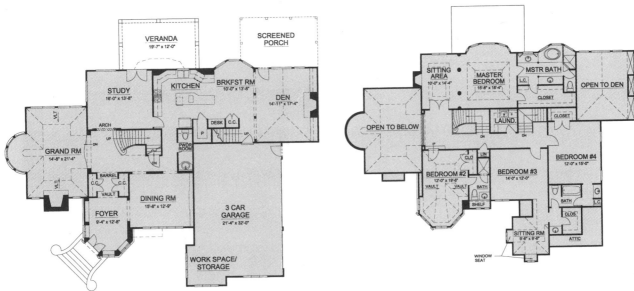

DESIGN HPT290053
©ARCHIVAL DESIGNS, INC.

DESIGN FEATURES

BEDROOMS: 4
BATHROOMS: 3½
FIRST FLOOR: 1,950 Sq. Ft.
SECOND FLOOR: 1,680 Sq. Ft.
TOTAL: 3,630 Sq. Ft.
WIDTH: 77'-0" DEPTH: 52'-0"

INTERESTING WINDOWS AND ROOFLINES give a unique character to this stucco facade. The European influences are unmistakable. To the right of the foyer, the study is highlighted by a beam ceiling, built-ins and floor-to-ceiling windows. The grand room is by itself to the left of the plan and includes a bayed sitting area and a fireplace. Another bay window brightens the breakfast room, which is found between the island kitchen and a den with a second fireplace. The living room and a grand stair hall complete the first floor. The elegant stairway leads up to three family bedrooms and a sumptuous master suite.

DESIGN FEATURES

BEDROOMS: 4

BATHROOMS: 3½

FIRST FLOOR: 2,032 Sq. Ft.

SECOND FLOOR: 1,028 Sq. Ft.

TOTAL: 3,060 Sq. Ft.

WIDTH: 55'-8" DEPTH: 62'-0"

THIS NARROW-LOT DESIGN would be ideal for a golf course or lakeside lot. Inside the arched entry, the formal dining room is separated from the foyer and the massive grand room by decorative pillars. At the end of the day, the family will enjoy gathering in the cozy keeping room with its fireplace and easy access to the large island kitchen and the sunny gazebo-style breakfast room. The master suite, located on the first floor for privacy, features a uniquely designed bedroom and a luxurious bath with His and Hers walk-in closets. Your family portraits and favorite art treasures can be displayed along the upstairs gallery, which shares space with three family bedrooms and two full baths.

DESIGN HPT290054
©ARCHIVAL DESIGNS, INC.

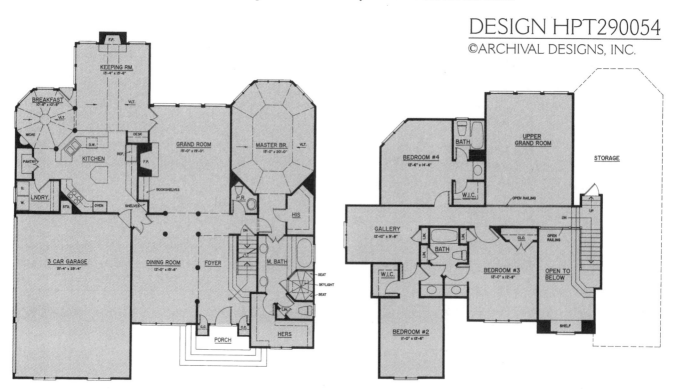

TURRETS, SCALLOPS, SPIRES AND COVERED PORCHES

combine to bring the historical Victorian era home to today's architectural

styles. Other features may include gable trim, tall narrow windows with

elaborate hooded crowns or "eyebrows" and fancy spindle-work, all in a

variety of combinations. Names like Gothic Revival and Queen Anne bring

to mind classical ideas, romance and a "dare-to-be-different" attitude.

Sophisticated homes offering both amenities and warmth fill a definite niche

in many neighborhoods, and help remind us that it's good to maintain pride

in oneself and one's surroundings. With spacious rooms, plenty of bay win-

dows and usually at least one welcoming covered porch, the homes featured

here present luxury not necessarily through size, but through quality.

SHOWN ABOVE:

DESIGN HPT290070 BY

LARRY E. BELK DESIGNS.

SEE PAGE 79 FOR MORE

INFORMATION ON

THIS GRACEFUL

VICTORIAN HOME

DESIGN HPT290055

DONALD A. GARDNER
ARCHITECTS, INC.

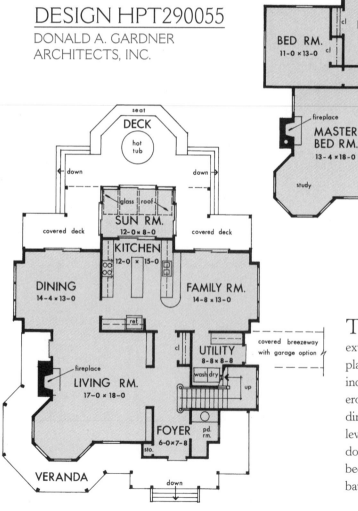

DESIGN FEATURES

BEDROOMS: 4
BATHROOMS: 3½
FIRST FLOOR: 1,393 Sq. Ft.
SECOND FLOOR: 1,195 Sq. Ft.
TOTAL: 2,588 Sq. Ft.
WIDTH: 44'-0" DEPTH: 50'-8"

THIS ELEGANT VICTORIAN home features an exterior of distinctive decorative detailing, yet offers an interior plan that satisfies today's standards. A spacious living room incorporates a large bay-windowed area and a fireplace. The generous kitchen with an island counter is centrally located to the dining and family rooms and to the sun room. On the second level, the master suite has a fireplace, walk-in closet and bay-windowed area which can serve as a study. Of the three additional bedrooms, one enjoys a private bath, while the others share a full bath. Plans for a separate garage are available if specified.

© 1986 Donald A. Gardner Architects, Inc.

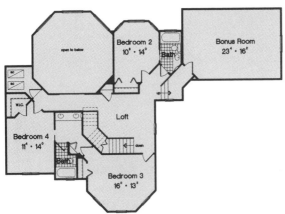

DESIGN HPT290056

©HOME DESIGN
SERVICES, INC.

THIS FARMHOUSE IS RESPLENDENT with Victorian detailing, from the pinnacle to the circular porch. The large dining room boasts a fabulous view to the front of the plan through a set of windows. Aspects of the family room that are sure to please include a fireplace and access to the rear covered porch. The kitchen area includes an island, nook, utility room and bathroom. The first-floor master suite contains His and Hers walk-in closets and dual vanities. Upstairs, three bedrooms share two full baths, and a bonus room completes the plan. The second-floor balcony looks to the family room below.

DESIGN FEATURES

BEDROOMS: 4
BATHROOMS: 3½
FIRST FLOOR: 2,041 Sq. Ft.
SECOND FLOOR: 1,098 Sq. Ft.
TOTAL: 3,139 Sq. Ft.
BONUS ROOM: 385 Sq. Ft.
WIDTH: 76'-6" DEPTH: 62'-2"

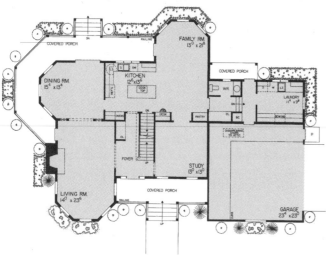

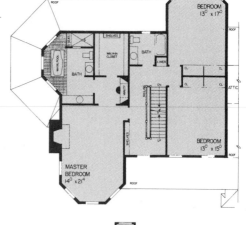

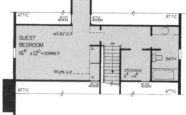

DESIGN HPT290057
©HOME PLANNERS

WHAT COULD BEAT THE CHARM of a turreted Victorian with covered porches to the front, side and rear? This delicately detailed exterior houses an outstanding family-oriented floor plan. Projecting bays make their contribution to the exterior styling. In addition, they provide an extra measure of livability to the living, dining and family rooms, plus two of the bedrooms. The efficient kitchen, with its island cooking station, functions well with the dining and family rooms. A study provides a quiet first-floor haven for the family's less active pursuits. Upstairs, there are three big bedrooms and a fine master bath. The third floor provides a guest suite and huge bulk storage area (make it a cedar closet if you wish). This house has a basement for the development of further recreational and storage facilities. Note the two fireplaces, large laundry and attached two-car garage.

DESIGN FEATURES
BEDROOMS: 4
BATHROOMS: 3½
FIRST FLOOR: 1,618 Sq. Ft.
SECOND FLOOR: 1,315 Sq. Ft.
THIRD FLOOR: 477 Sq. Ft.
TOTAL: 3,410 Sq. Ft.
WIDTH: 71'-8" DEPTH: 48'-4"

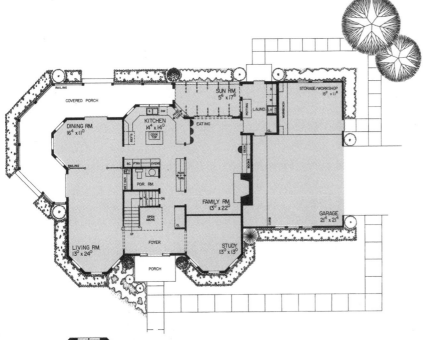

Quote One®

Cost to build? See page 186
to order complete cost estimate
to build this house in your area!

DESIGN FEATURES

BEDROOMS: 4

BATHROOMS: 2½

FIRST FLOOR: 1,766 Sq. Ft.

SECOND FLOOR: 1,519 Sq. Ft.

TOTAL: 3,285 Sq. Ft.

WIDTH: 77'-7" DEPTH: 44'-2"

L

DESIGN HPT290058
©HOME PLANNERS

THE STATELY PROPORTIONS and exquisite Victorian detailing of this home are exciting indeed. Like so many Victorian houses, interesting rooflines set the character of this design. Observe the delightful mixture of gabled roof, hipped roof and dramatic turret. The kitchen features a center island cooktop and shares a wide counter for casual dining with the adjoining family room. A bayed dining room with access to the rear porch is available for more formal occasions. Upstairs, each of the four bedrooms offers a bay area and plenty of closet space. Don't miss the spacious master bath.

DESIGN HPT290059
©HOME PLANNERS

THE MOST POPULAR FEATURE of the Victorian house has always been its covered porches. The two finely detailed outdoor living spaces on this home add much to formal and informal entertaining options. However, in addition to its wonderful Victorian facade, this home provides a myriad of interior features that cater to the active, growing family. Living and dining areas include a formal living room and dining room, a family room with a fireplace, a study and a kitchen with an attached breakfast nook. The second floor contains three family bedrooms and a luxurious master suite with a whirlpool spa and His and Hers walk-in closets.

DESIGN FEATURES

BEDROOMS: 4

BATHROOMS: 2½

FIRST FLOOR: 1,269 Sq. Ft.

SECOND FLOOR: 1,227 Sq. Ft.

TOTAL: 2,496 Sq. Ft.

WIDTH: 70'-0" DEPTH: 44'-5"

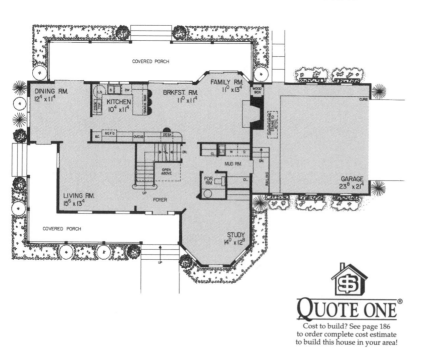

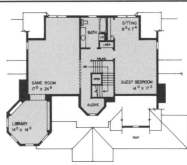

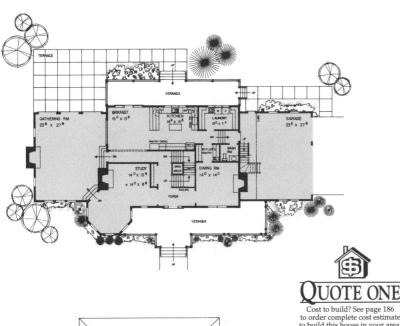

QUOTE ONE®

Cost to build? See page 186
to order complete cost estimate
to build this house in your area!

DESIGN FEATURES

BEDROOMS: 5

BATHROOMS: 3½

FIRST FLOOR: 2,248 Sq. Ft.

SECOND FLOOR: 2,020 Sq. Ft.

THIRD FLOOR: 1,117 Sq. Ft.

TOTAL: 5,385 Sq. Ft.

WIDTH: 94'-7" DEPTH: 53'-4"

L D

DESIGN HPT290060
©HOME PLANNERS

THIS HOME IS A LOVELY EXAMPLE of classic
Queen Anne architecture. Its floor plan offers a gathering room with
a fireplace, a study with an octagonal window area, a formal dining
room and a kitchen with an attached breakfast room. Bedrooms on
the second floor include three family bedrooms and a grand master
suite. On the third floor are a guest room with a private bath and sitting room and a game room an with attached library.

DESIGN HPT290061
©HOME PLANNERS

THIS HOME IS PERFECT for a narrow in-fill lot in a neighborhood with an architectural history. A simple but charming Queen Anne Victorian, this enchanting three-story home includes a living room with a fireplace, a large family kitchen with a snack bar and a second fireplace, and a dining room with a nearby wet bar. The second floor holds two bedrooms, one a master suite with a grand bath. A tucked-away guest suite on the third floor has a private bath.

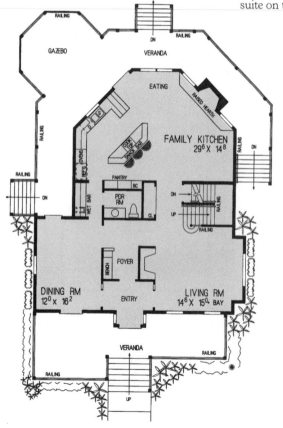

Quote One®
Cost to build? See page 186 to order complete cost estimate to build this house in your area!

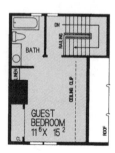

DESIGN FEATURES

BEDROOMS: 3

BATHROOMS: 3½

FIRST FLOOR: 1,366 Sq. Ft.

SECOND FLOOR: 837 Sq. Ft.

THIRD FLOOR: 363 Sq. Ft.

TOTAL: 2,566 Sq. Ft.

WIDTH: 50'-2" DEPTH: 69'-3"

L D

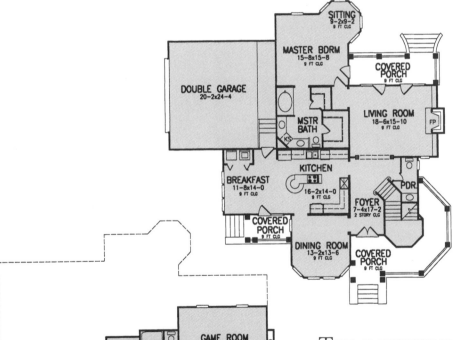

DESIGN HPT290062
©LARRY E. BELK DESIGNS

THE IMPRESSIVE ENTRANCE of this Victorian home welcomes guests to the formal areas—the dining room to the left and the living room straight ahead. The covered porch opening off the living room provides a pleasant sitting space in warm weather, while a fireplace is appreciated on cool evenings. A side-porch entry opens to the breakfast room. On this level, the master suite offers a sitting bay, two walk-in closets, a bath with separate vanities and a private entrance from the rear porch. Two bedrooms upstairs share a bath and a game room. Each bedroom includes a private balcony and a walk-in closet. Please specify crawlspace or slab foundation when ordering.

DESIGN HPT290063

DONALD A. GARDNER
ARCHITECTS, INC.

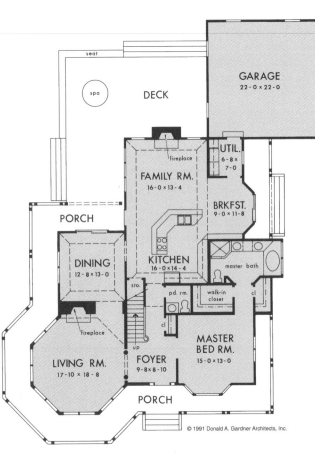

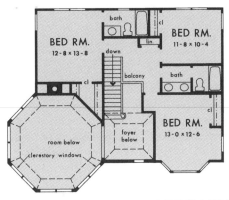

© 1991 Donald A. Gardner Architects, Inc.

DESIGN FEATURES

BEDROOMS: 4

BATHROOMS: 3½

FIRST FLOOR: 1,790 Sq. Ft.

SECOND FLOOR: 792 Sq. Ft.

TOTAL: 2,582 Sq. Ft.

WIDTH: 63'-0" DEPTH: 80'-4"

AN EXTENSIVE WRAPAROUND PORCH and a luxurious deck dramatically increase the living space of this quintessential farmhouse. The foyer opens to the master suite and a glorious two-story living room that offers stupendous views and a cozy fireplace. The kitchen with an island work space serves the formal dining room and sunny breakfast nook. The master suite includes a walk-in closet and bath with a double-bowl vanity, shower and garden tub. The second floor consists of three bedrooms: one has a private bath while the other two share a full bath.

DESIGN HPT290064

©ALAN MASCORD DESIGN
ASSOCIATES, INC.

DESIGN FEATURES

BEDROOMS: 3

BATHROOMS: 2½

FIRST FLOOR: 1,337 Sq. Ft.

SECOND FLOOR: 1,025 Sq. Ft.

TOTAL: 2,362 Sq. Ft.

WIDTH: 50'-6" DEPTH: 72'-6"

AN OCTAGONAL TOWER, fish-scale shingles and a wrap-around porch lend a true Victorian flavor to this impressive plan. More than just a pretty face, the turret houses a spacious den with built-in cabinetry on the first floor, and provides a sunny bay window for a family bedroom upstairs. Just off the foyer, the formal living and dining rooms create an elegant open space for entertaining, while a focal-point fireplace with an extended hearth warms up a spacious family area. The cooktop-island kitchen and morning nook lead to a powder room and laundry area. Two second-floor bedrooms share a full bath, while the master suite offers a private bath with an oversized whirlpool tub, twin vanities and a walk-in closet.

DESIGN HPT290065
©HOME PLANNERS

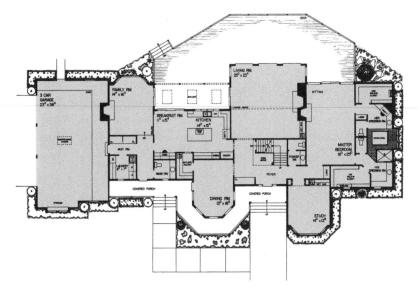

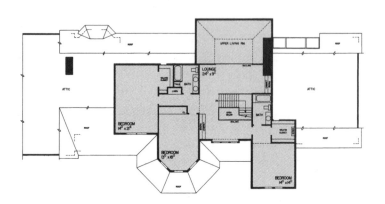

THIS ENCHANTING MANOR displays architectural elements typical of the Victorian style: asymmetrical facade, decorative shingles and gables, and a covered porch. The two-story living room with a fireplace and wet bar opens to the glass-enclosed rear porch with skylights. A spacious kitchen is filled with amenities, including an island cooktop, built-in desk, and butler's pantry connecting to the dining room. The master suite, adjacent to the study, opens to the rear deck; a cozy fireplace keeps the room warm on chilly evenings. Separate His and Hers dressing rooms are outfitted with vanities and walk-in closets, and a luxurious whirlpool tub connects the baths. The second floor opens to a large lounge with built-in cabinets and bookshelves. Three bedrooms and two full baths complete the second-floor living arrangements. The three-car garage contains disappearing stairs to an attic storage area.

DESIGN FEATURES
BEDROOMS: 4
BATHROOMS: 4½ + ½
FIRST FLOOR: 3,079 Sq. Ft.
SECOND FLOOR: 1,461 Sq. Ft.
TOTAL: 4,540 Sq. Ft.
WIDTH: 118'-4" DEPTH: 54'-6"

L

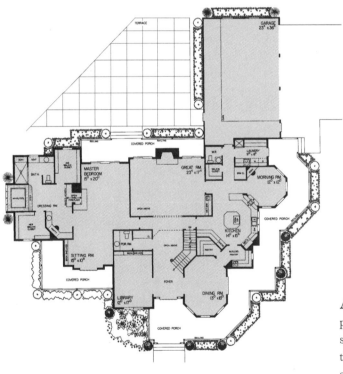

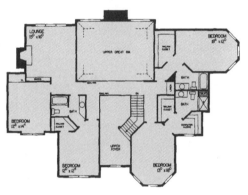

DESIGN HPT290066
©HOME PLANNERS

A MAGNIFICENT, FINELY WROUGHT covered porch wraps around this impressive Victorian estate home. The two-story foyer provides a direct view past the stylish banister and into the great room with a large central fireplace. To the left of the foyer is a bookshelf-lined library and to the right is an octagonal-shaped dining room. The island cooktop completes a convenient work triangle in the kitchen and a pass-through connects this room with the morning room. A butler's pantry, walk-in closet and broom closet offer plenty of storage space. A luxurious master suite on the first floor opens to the rear covered porch. A through-fireplace warms the bedroom, sitting room and dressing room, which includes His and Hers walk-in closets. Four uniquely designed bedrooms, three full baths and a lounge with a fireplace are located on the second floor.

DESIGN FEATURES

BEDROOMS: 5
BATHROOMS: 4½ + ½
FIRST FLOOR: 2,995 Sq. Ft.
SECOND FLOOR: 1,831 Sq. Ft.
TOTAL: 4,826 Sq. Ft.
WIDTH: 95'-0" DEPTH: 99'-3"

L|D

VICTORIAN ELEGANCE

DESIGN HPT290067
©DESIGN BASICS, INC.

THE INTRICATE DETAILING, tall brick chimney, and stately veranda on the elevation of this four-bedroom, 1½-story home blend effortlessly into Victorian elegance. Other preferred features include the two-story entrance hall, a bay window in the formal dining room, the open island kitchen with a pantry and desk, the private master suite with a vaulted ceiling, and the two-person whirlpool tub in the master bath. This versatile plan is designed for practical living, with guest rooms or children's bedrooms located on the upper level. One of these second-story bedrooms features a walk-in closet.

DESIGN FEATURES

BEDROOMS: 4
BATHROOMS: 2½
FIRST FLOOR: 1,553 Sq. Ft.
SECOND FLOOR: 725 Sq. Ft.
TOTAL: 2,278 Sq. Ft.
WIDTH: 54'-0" DEPTH: 50'-0"

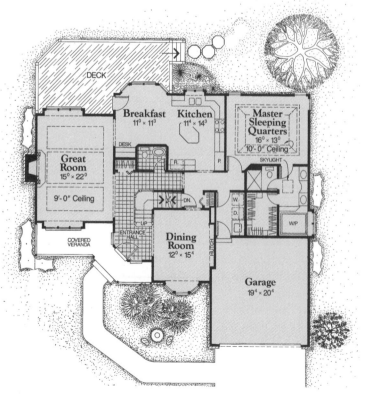

DESIGN FEATURES

BEDROOMS: 4

BATHROOMS: 2½

FIRST FLOOR: 1,308 Sq. Ft.

SECOND FLOOR: 1,107 Sq. Ft.

TOTAL: 2,415 Sq. Ft.

WIDTH: 54'-0" DEPTH: 42'-0"

DESIGN HPT290068

©DESIGN BASICS, INC.

EMBELLISHED WITH INTERESTING detail, this four-bedroom, two-story home offers an alternative to the ordinary. The covered veranda welcomes all to a marvelous floor plan. Thoughtful amenities include a dining room with added hutch space, a bay window in the parlor, a large gathering room with a fireplace and plenty of windows and a featured-filled kitchen. The luxurious master bedroom has a vaulted ceiling and pampering bath with a whirlpool tub, double lavatories, and two closets. Upstairs, three secondary bedrooms share a full bath that includes double lavatories.

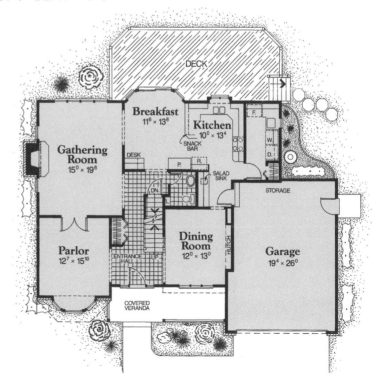

DESIGN FEATURES

BEDROOMS: 5

BATHROOMS: 3½

FIRST FLOOR: 1,538 Sq. Ft.

SECOND FLOOR: 1,526 Sq. Ft.

THIRD FLOOR: 658 Sq. Ft.

TOTAL: 3,722 Sq. Ft.

WIDTH: 67'-0" DEPTH: 66'-0"

L

DESIGN HPT290069
©HOME PLANNERS

THIS CHARMING VICTORIAN HOME is reminiscent of a time when letter writing was an art and the scent of lavender hung lightly in the air. However, the floor plan moves quickly into the present with a contemporary flair. A veranda wraps around the living room, providing entrance from each side. The hub of the first floor is a kitchen that serves the dining room, the family room and the living room with equal ease. Located on the second floor are two family bedrooms, a full bath and an opulent master suite. Amenities in this suite include a fireplace, a bay-windowed sitting room, a pampering master bath and a private sun deck. The third floor holds two bedrooms—one a possible study—and a full bath.

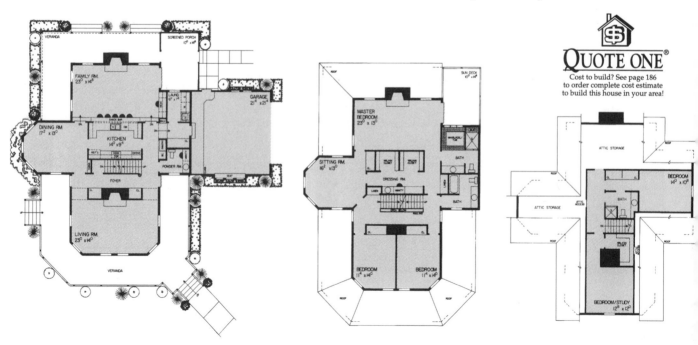

Quote One®

Cost to build? See page 186 to order complete cost estimate to build this house in your area!

DESIGN FEATURES

BEDROOMS: 3

BATHROOMS: 2½

FIRST FLOOR: 2,194 Sq. Ft.

SECOND FLOOR: 870 Sq. Ft.

TOTAL: 3,064 Sq. Ft.

BONUS ROOM: 251 Sq. Ft.

WIDTH: 50'-11" DEPTH: 91'-2"

DESIGN HPT290070
©LARRY E. BELK DESIGNS

WITH EQUALLY APPEALING FRONT and side entrances, a charming Victorian facade invites entry to this stunning home. The foyer showcases the characteristic winding staircase and opens to the large great room with a masonry fireplace. An enormous kitchen features a cooktop island and a breakfast bar large enough to seat four. A lovely bay window distinguishes the nearby dining room. The master suite with another masonry fireplace is located on the first floor. The amenity-filled private bath features double vanities, a whirlpool tub, a separate shower and a gigantic walk-in closet with an additional cedar closet. The second floor contains two bedrooms—one with access to the outdoor balcony on the side of the home. The third floor is completely expandable. Please specify crawlspace or slab foundation when ordering.

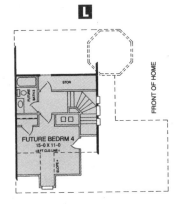

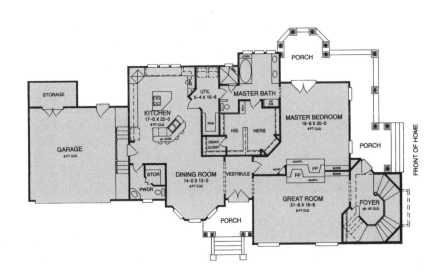

DESIGN HPT290071

©DESIGN BASICS, INC.

SPECIAL WINDOW DETAILING and a gaze-bo veranda highlight the exterior of this charming home. From the entry, French doors open to an elegant drawing room with a spider-beam ceiling. The dining room, with hutch space and a bay window, suits entertaining needs. In the gathering room, three repeating arch windows, a fireplace and two bookcases form a comfortable retreat. The island kitchen features two pantries, a planning desk and wrapping counters. The curved staircase leads to upper-level sleeping quarters. The impressive master suite enjoys a tiered ceiling, a massive wardrobe and dressing area, and a private bath. Three family bedrooms—two with window seats—share a full bath.

DESIGN FEATURES

BEDROOMS: 4

BATHROOMS: 2½

FIRST FLOOR: 1,249 Sq. Ft.

SECOND FLOOR: 1,075 Sq. Ft.

TOTAL: 2,324 Sq. Ft.

WIDTH: 56'-0" DEPTH: 46'-0"

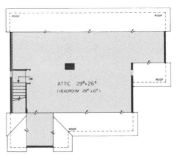

Quote One®
Cost to build? See page 186
to order complete cost estimate
to build this house in your area!

DESIGN HPT290072

©HOME PLANNERS

COVERED PORCHES, FRONT AND BACK, are a fine preview to the liv-
able nature of this Victorian design. Living areas are defined in a family room with a fireplace, formal living and dining rooms and a kitchen with a breakfast room. An ample laundry room, a garage with a storage area, and a powder room round out the first floor. Three second-floor bedrooms are joined by a study and two full baths. The master suite on this floor has two closets, including an ample walk-in, as well as a relaxing bath with a tile-rimmed whirlpool tub and a separate shower with a seat.

DESIGN FEATURES

BEDROOMS: 3
BATHROOMS: 2½
FIRST FLOOR: 1,375 Sq. Ft.
SECOND FLOOR: 1,016 Sq. Ft.
TOTAL: 2,391 Sq. Ft.
BONUS ROOM: 303 Sq. Ft.
WIDTH: 62'-7" DEPTH: 54'-0"

THIS ROMANTIC FARMHOUSE, with its open living spaces, covered porches and decorative widow's walk, is designed with gracious family living in mind. From the lovely wraparound porch, the foyer first meets the front parlor through an arched doorway. The impressive formal dining room just beyond will be a delight for casual meals as well as formal affairs. The grand room takes center stage with rear-porch access, a corner fireplace, built-in media center and pass-through to the kitchen. The kitchen features a work island, eating counter and breakfast nook. The master suite is lavishly appointed with a spa-style bath, a sitting area and private access to the rear porch. Upstairs, a computer loft with built-ins serves as a common area to the three family bedrooms that share a full hall bath. Please specify basement or slab foundation when ordering.

DESIGN HPT290073
©THE SATER DESIGN
COLLECTION

DESIGN FEATURES

BEDROOMS: 4

BATHROOMS: 2½

FIRST FLOOR: 2,240 Sq. Ft.

SECOND FLOOR: 943 Sq. Ft.

TOTAL: 3,183 Sq. Ft.

WIDTH: 69'-8" DEPTH: 61'-10"

WHEN ONE THINKS OF COUNTRY LIVING,

the images that usually come to mind include covered wraparound porches,

shuttered windows and at least one fireplace to warm up cool fall evenings.

Spacious kitchens where the family can gather to talk about the day and a

general feeling of sturdiness and welcome are also common. Country abodes

tend to feature dormers, horizontal siding, double-pitched rooflines and

multi-pane windows. A family room is generally brightened by a fireplace,

and the kids' bedrooms are usually separated from the master suite. Here in

our collection, the definition of luxury is having plenty of room for the fami-

ly to spread out and enjoy the home. Yet, these homes still manage to main-

tain a down-home country ambiance, even with all the extra amenities.

SHOWN ABOVE:

DESIGN HPT290075

BY FRANK BETZ

ASSOCIATES, INC.

SEE PAGE 85 FOR

MORE INFORMATION

ON THIS CLASSIC

COUNTRY HOME.

DESIGN HPT290074
©LARRY E. BELK DESIGNS

THIS TWO-STORY TREASURE will enhance any neighborhood with its complex rooflines, while the interior will delight with its open and angular design. The grand foyer, with its centerpiece staircase, opens to the three main living spaces. The dining, living and breakfast/keeping rooms are gracefully defined by columns and arches. The large island kitchen is well positioned between the breakfast/keeping and dining rooms. Wrapping around the garage are the exercise and game rooms, a toy closet, full bath, utility room and a secondary stairway. The second floor boasts three family bedrooms, the master suite and a hobby room. The master suite offers a sitting area that opens to a private sun deck.

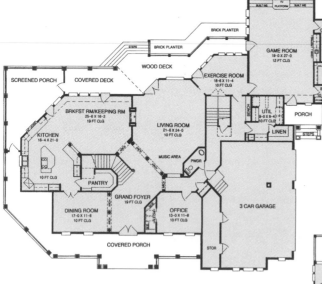

DESIGN FEATURES

BEDROOMS: 4

BATHROOMS: 4½

FIRST FLOOR: 3,477 Sq. Ft.

SECOND FLOOR: 2,577 Sq. Ft.

TOTAL: 6,054 Sq. Ft.

WIDTH: 100'-5" DEPTH: 78'-8"

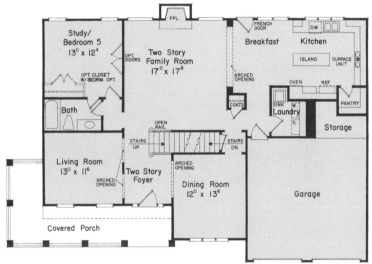

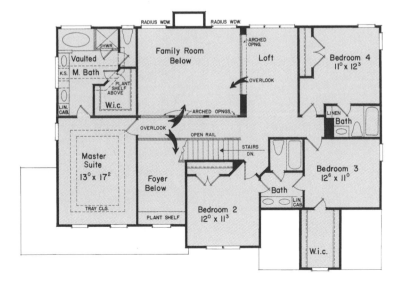

DESIGN HPT290075

©FRANK BETZ
ASSOCIATES, INC.

THIS FIVE-BEDROOM HOME will look wonderful in any neighborhood! An island country kitchen with an adjacent breakfast room will be one of many highlights of this two-story traditional home. The kitchen connects to the formal dining room, which is accessible via an arched opening from the two-story foyer. The central family room includes a fireplace flanked by windows. Upstairs the master suite enjoys a luxurious bath with a walk-in closet and a corner whirlpool tub. Three bedrooms and a loft overlooking the family room complete the second floor. Please specify basement or crawlspace foundation when ordering.

DESIGN FEATURES

BEDROOMS: 5

BATHROOMS: 3½

FIRST FLOOR: 1,426 Sq. Ft.

SECOND FLOOR: 1,408 Sq. Ft.

TOTAL: 2,834 Sq. Ft.

WIDTH: 60'-0" DEPTH: 41'-4"

ASYMMETRICAL GABLES AND A PEDIMENTED ENTRY sup-

ported by double columns lend visual interest to this blended exterior. Inside, the wrap-around hallway opens to the living and dining rooms and the family room. The gourmet kitchen easily serves the formal dining room and conveniently opens to the family room. The master suite is tucked into a private corner of the plan. Two spacious second-floor bedrooms share a full bath. A third family bedroom has a private bath which makes it a perfect choice for use as a guest suite. This home is designed with a basement foundation.

DESIGN FEATURES

BEDROOMS: 4
BATHROOMS: 3½
FIRST FLOOR: 2,012 Sq. Ft.
SECOND FLOOR: 1,254 Sq. Ft.
TOTAL: 3,266 Sq. Ft.
WIDTH: 70'-0" DEPTH: 75'-6"

DESIGN HPT290076
©STEPHEN FULLER, INC.

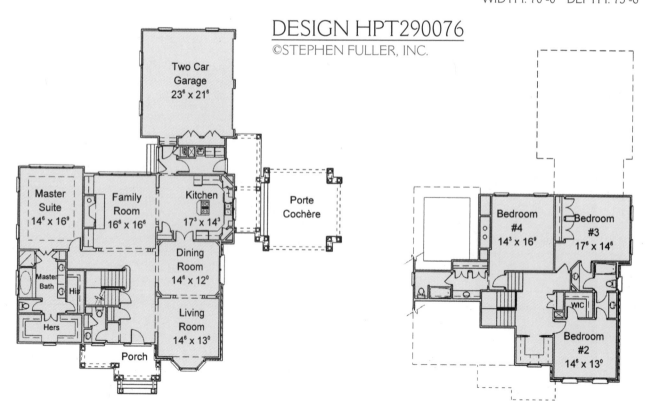

DESIGN FEATURES

BEDROOMS: 4

BATHROOMS: 3½

FIRST FLOOR: 1,437 Sq. Ft.

SECOND FLOOR: 1,747 Sq. Ft.

TOTAL: 3,184 Sq. Ft.

WIDTH: 56'-0" DEPTH: 68'-2"

DESIGN HPT290077
©STEPHEN FULLER, INC.

THIS HOME SKILLFULLY BLENDS formal design with the warmth and texture of Farmhouse style. Mixing traditional materials such as brick and clapboard makes a beautiful statement in today's comfortable neighborhoods. Inside, a winding staircase is the focal point of the foyer. The living room, gently lit by a bay window, opens to the formal dining room. The great room offers a fireplace and French doors to the rear porch. Upstairs, a gallery hall provides space for a study area or reading nook. A lovely master suite features a cozy sitting area, twin walk-in closets and an opulent bath. Three additional bedrooms, one with a walk-in closet, and two full baths finish up the second floor. This home is designed with a basement foundation.

THIS ENGAGING DESIGN BLENDS the clean, sharp edges of the sophisticated shingle style with relaxed cottage details such as dovecoat gables and flower boxes. The rear of the plan takes advantage of rows of windows, allowing great views. The great room, with built-in bookshelves and a fireplace, opens to the kitchen and breakfast room, where a door leads to the deck. A spacious guest bedroom, also with access to the deck, has an adjoining bath and a walk-in closet. Upstairs, a study area provides a built-in desk. A dramatic master suite includes a bath with double vanities, a garden tub and a separate shower. Two bedrooms, one with a walk-in closet, share a full bath, while a third features a private bath. This home is designed with a walkout basement foundation

DESIGN HPT290078
©STEPHEN FULLER, INC.

DESIGN FEATURES

BEDROOMS: 5
BATHROOMS: 4½
FIRST FLOOR: 1,527 Sq. Ft.
SECOND FLOOR: 1,680 Sq. Ft.
TOTAL: 3,207 Sq. Ft.
WIDTH: 63'-6" DEPTH: 62'-6"

THIS STONE-AND-SHINGLE FACADE complements a gambrel roof, while a Chippendale parapet resides atop the porte cochere and displays an intricately detailed railing. Inside, a well-arranged interior features a center passageway with a straight stair running from front to back. On the first floor, the formal living/dining room leads to a side entry. On the right, the expansive great room features a massive hearth and access to a covered rear deck. The family will share casual meals in the breakfast room adjoining the kitchen. The upper floor includes four bedrooms, one an extravagant master suite with two walk-in closets. Bedrooms 2 and 3 share a full bath, while Bedroom 4 has a private bath and two wall closets. This home is designed with a basement foundation.

DESIGN FEATURES

BEDROOMS: 4
BATHROOMS: 3½
FIRST FLOOR: 1,635 Sq. Ft.
SECOND FLOOR: 1,974 Sq. Ft.
TOTAL: 3,609 Sq. Ft.
WIDTH: 70'-6" DEPTH: 77'-4"

DESIGN HPT290079
©STEPHEN FULLER, INC.

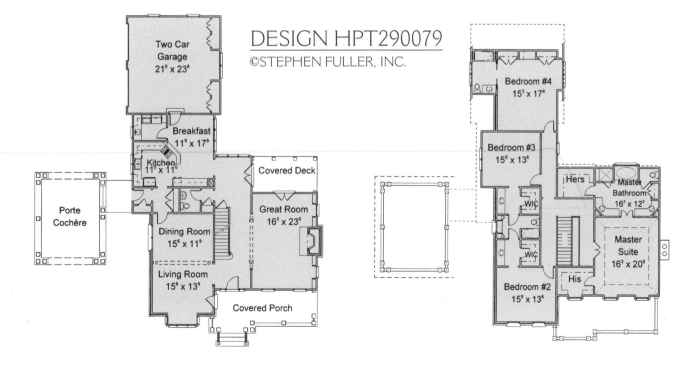

COUNTRY ABUNDANCE

DESIGN FEATURES

BEDROOMS: 4

BATHROOMS: 2½

TOTAL: 2,465 Sq. Ft.

WIDTH: 65'-1" DEPTH: 64'-2"

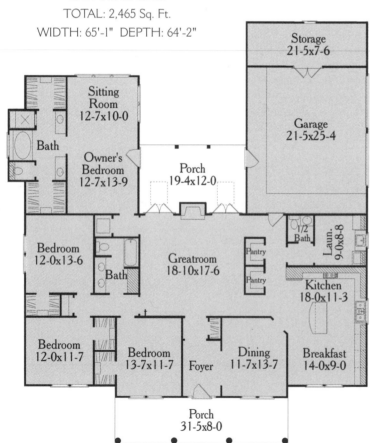

DESIGN HPT290080

©LARRY JAMES & ASSOCIATES, INC.

AN INVITING FRONT PORCH welcomes visitors into this enchanting home. The central great room features a gorgeous fireplace with double doors on each side leading to the skylit rear porch. The formal dining room to the right of the foyer provides an angled entrance to the kitchen. The L-shaped kitchen has an incredible countertop area and a central island for even more work space. A breakfast area and twin pantries complete the kitchen area. The master suite includes a large sitting area, a deluxe private bath and His and Hers walk-in closets. Three family bedrooms complete the sleeping area; all three feature walk-in closets. Please specify basement, crawlspace or slab foundation when ordering.

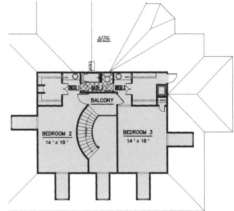

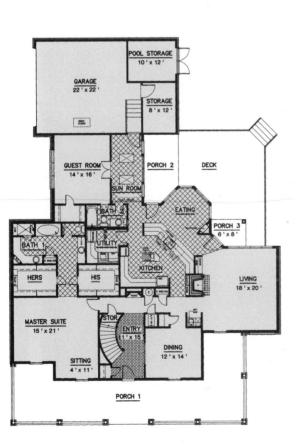

DESIGN HPT290081

©BRELAND & FARMER
DESIGNERS, INC.

HERE IS A WONDERFUL CONTEMPORARY home with three porches that is perfect for warmer climates or vacation property. A stunning circular staircase is the centerpiece of the foyer. The kitchen is ideal for the chef in the family with its island work area and expansive counter space. The dining room connects to the kitchen by a butler's pantry. The living room provides a warming fireplace and access to a porch. A skylit sun room leads to a guest room through French doors. Two family bedrooms and a full bath are on the second level, while the master suite is secluded for privacy on the first level. Please specify crawlspace or slab foundation when ordering.

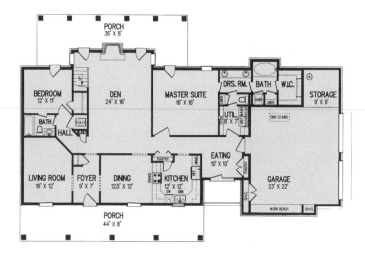

DESIGN HPT290082

©BRELAND & FARMER
DESIGNERS, INC.

THIS FOUR-BEDROOM, traditional beauty possesses the quaint look of an older home. The two-story den includes a fireplace and a large rear porch accessible via French doors. The kitchen has a large pantry and is located directly between the eating area and the formal dining room. The master suite is situated for convenience and features a plush bath. The three bedrooms on the upper level all have huge walk-in closets and are accessed by a stairwell that is open to the den. Please specify crawlspace or slab foundation when ordering.

DESIGN FEATURES

BEDROOMS: 5
BATHROOMS: 4
FIRST FLOOR: 1,925 Sq. Ft.
SECOND FLOOR: 1,134 Sq. Ft.
TOTAL: 3,059 Sq. Ft.
WIDTH: 78'-0" DEPTH: 52'-0"

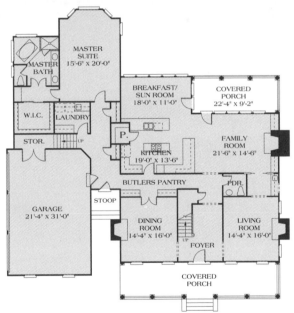

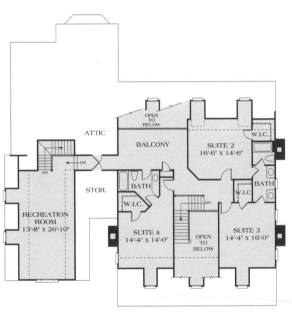

DESIGN HPT290083

©LIVING CONCEPTS
HOME PLANNING

THIS CHARMING TWO-STORY HOME offers the warmth of three fire-places. The foyer is flanked by the dining room on the left and the living room on the right, both of which boast a fireplace. Service to the dining room from the large island kitchen is made simple with the benefits of the butler's pantry. The breakfast/sun room is ideal for casual dining and offers access to the covered porch. The family room features a wall of windows and a fireplace with built-ins and also provides covered-porch access. The luxurious master suite is isolated for privacy and presents a private bath and walk-in closet. Three additional suites are situated on the second floor along with a recreational room over the garage.

DESIGN FEATURES

BEDROOMS: 4
BATHROOMS: 3½
FIRST FLOOR: 2,647 Sq. Ft.
SECOND FLOOR: 1,372 Sq. Ft.
TOTAL: 4,019 Sq. Ft.
BONUS ROOM: 453 Sq. Ft.
WIDTH: 72'-10" DEPTH: 71'-8"

DESIGN FEATURES

BEDROOMS: 4

BATHROOMS: 3½

FIRST FLOOR: 1,679 Sq. Ft.

SECOND FLOOR: 1,990 Sq. Ft.

TOTAL: 3,669 Sq. Ft.

WIDTH: 75'-2" DEPTH: 65'-0"

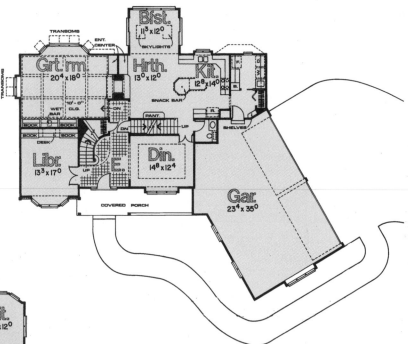

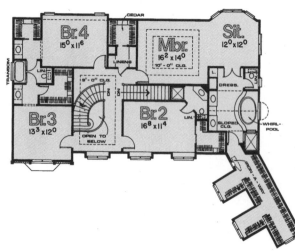

DESIGN HPT290084
©DESIGN BASICS, INC.

BEAUTIFUL WINDOWS bring the outdoors in throughout this home. French doors lead into the library with a bayed window, built-in desk and bookcases. Homeowners will relish the combination breakfast/hearth room and kitchen concept. Special finishing touches include the bayed sitting area in the master suite, the beam ceiling in the great room and the box-bay window in the dining room. The master dressing/bath area is enhanced by His and Hers vanities, an oval whirlpool tub beneath the arched window and a deluxe walk-in closet with windows.

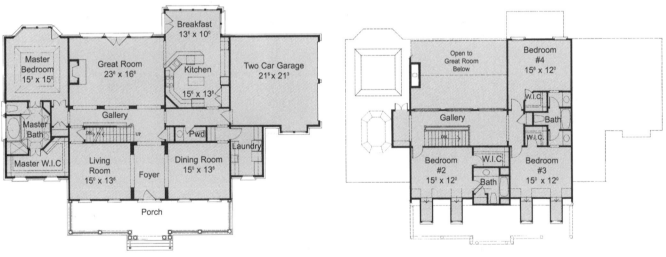

DESIGN HPT290085

©STEPHEN FULLER, INC.

THIS GRAND HOME DISPLAYS the finest in farmhouse design. Dormer windows and a traditional brick and siding exterior create a welcoming facade. Inside, the entry foyer opens to a formal zone consisting of a living room to the left and a dining room to the right. The kitchen enjoys a pass-through to the breakfast area—the great room is just a step away. Here, a fireplace graces the far end of the room while a wall of glass allows light to penetrate the interior of the room. Double doors grant passage to the backyard. Beyond the first-floor gallery, the master bedroom boasts a tray ceiling, a window bay and a lavish bath. Upstairs, three family bedrooms all have walk-in closets and direct access to a bath. This home is designed with a basement foundation.

DESIGN FEATURES

BEDROOMS: 4
BATHROOMS: 3½
FIRST FLOOR: 2,315 Sq. Ft.
SECOND FLOOR: 1,200 Sq. Ft.
TOTAL: 3,515 Sq. Ft.
WIDTH: 77'-4" DEPTH: 46'-8"

DESIGN HPT290086

©STEPHEN FULLER, INC.

DESIGN FEATURES

BEDROOMS: 4

BATHROOMS: 3½

FIRST FLOOR: 2,155 Sq. Ft.

SECOND FLOOR: 1,020 Sq. Ft.

TOTAL: 3,175 Sq. Ft.

BONUS ROOM: 262 Sq. Ft.

WIDTH: 62'-0" DEPTH: 63'-0"

To HIGHLIGHT THE EXTERIOR of this home, wood siding and paneled shutters are artfully combined with arched transoms, gables and a sweeping roofline to define the beautiful glass entry. The open foyer at once reveals the large living and dining rooms and a classic great room with a coffered ceiling and hearth. Double doors open to the master suite with a unique tray ceiling and fireplace. The private bath includes double vanities, a shower, corner garden tub and His and Hers closets. The exercise room can be accessed from either the master suite or great room and opens to the porch at the rear of the home. The generous corner breakfast area also opens to the porch. The large kitchen with a cooktop island, pantry and the laundry room complete the main level. The gallery features built-in bookshelves and a computer/study nook with easy access from all three bedrooms on the upper level. This home is designed with a walkout basement foundation.

©1998 Donald A. Gardner, Inc.

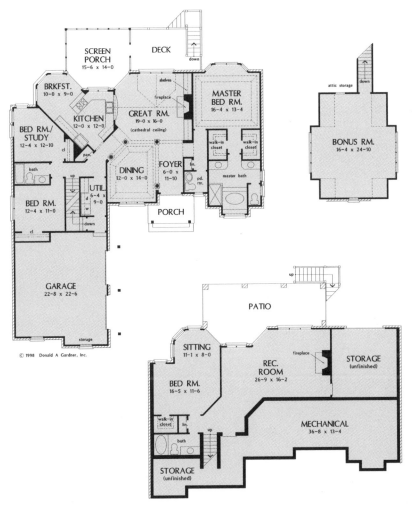

© 1998 Donald A Gardner, Inc.

SCREEN PORCH 15-6 x 14-0

DECK

down

BRKFST. 10-0 x 9-0

KITCHEN 12-0 x 12-0

shelves

fireplace

GREAT RM. 19-0 x 16-0
(cathedral ceiling)

MASTER BED RM. 16-4 x 13-4

walk-in closet

walk-in closet

master bath

BED RM./ STUDY 12-4 x 12-10

cl

pan.

up

DINING 12-0 x 14-0

FOYER 6-0 x 11-10

lin.

pd. rm.

UTIL. 6-4 x 9-0

d

w

PORCH

bath

BED RM. 12-4 x 11-0

cl

down

GARAGE 22-8 x 22-6

storage

attic storage

down

BONUS RM. 16-4 x 24-10

up

PATIO

SITTING 11-1 x 8-0

REC. ROOM 26-9 x 16-2

fireplace

STORAGE (unfinished)

BED RM. 16-5 x 11-6

walk-in closet

lin.

up

bath

MECHANICAL 36-8 x 13-4

STORAGE (unfinished)

DESIGN HPT290087

DONALD A. GARDNER ARCHITECTS, INC.

A PARTIAL BASEMENT foundation makes this home perfect for hillside lots, while its mixture of exterior building materials and Craftsman details gives it the look of a custom design. The great room features a cathedral ceiling, fireplace with built-in shelves and access to the screened porch. The master suite occupies a wing all its own an includes a bay window, twin walk-in closets and an impressive bath with dual vanities, garden tub and shower. On the other side of the plan, two family bedrooms sit behind the two-car garage, near the galley kitchen and bayed breakfast room. Downstairs, a rec room and another bedroom with a sitting area open to a patio.

DESIGN FEATURES

BEDROOMS: 4

BATHROOMS: 3½

MAIN LEVEL: 2,094 Sq. Ft.

FINISHED BASEMENT: 1,038 Sq. Ft.

TOTAL: 3,132 Sq. Ft.

BONUS ROOM: 494 Sq. Ft.

WIDTH: 62'-3" DEPTH: 76'-7"

COUNTRY ABUNDANCE

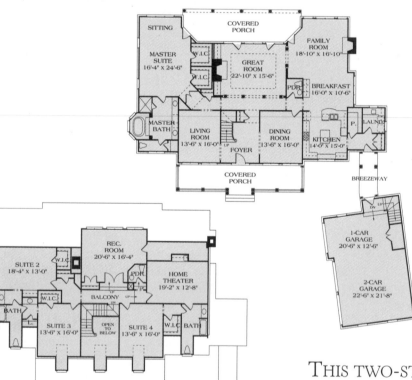

DESIGN FEATURES

BEDROOMS: 4

BATHROOMS: 3½ + ½

FIRST FLOOR: 2,920 Sq. Ft.

SECOND FLOOR: 2,186 Sq. Ft.

TOTAL: 5,106 Sq. Ft.

BONUS ROOM: 564 Sq. Ft.

WIDTH: 86'-7" DEPTH: 103'-6"

DESIGN HPT290088
©LIVING CONCEPTS
HOME PLANNING

THIS TWO-STORY HOME OFFERS an unfinished area over the unattached, three-car garage that would be suitable for a future apartment or private study. Past the foyer's centerpiece staircase, to the great room opens up with its tray ceiling, fireplace and window wall accessing the rear covered porch. The secluded master suite offers a sunny sitting area that also accesses the rear porch. The dining room, breakfast nook and island kitchen are all positioned for efficiency with nearby utility room. A rec room and home theater share the second floor with three additional suites and two full baths.

DESIGN HPT290089

DONALD A. GARDNER
ARCHITECTS, INC.

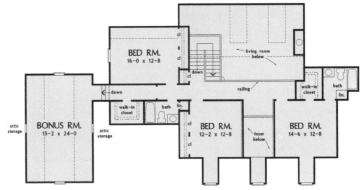

TEEMING WITH LUXURY and style, this gracious country estate features spacious rooms, volume ceilings and four porches for extended outdoor living. Fireplaces in the living and family rooms grant warmth and character to these spacious gathering areas, while columns add definition to the open living and dining rooms. Built-in bookshelves in the living room are both attractive and functional, as is the built-in desk adjacent to the open, U-shaped staircase. The master suite is more haven than bedroom with a tray ceiling, sitting alcove, dual walk-in closets and a luxurious bath. The upstairs balcony overlooks both the foyer and living room while serving as an open, central hallway for the home's three family bedrooms and bonus room.

DESIGN FEATURES

BEDROOMS: 4

BATHROOMS: 3½

FIRST FLOOR: 2,676 Sq. Ft.

SECOND FLOOR: 1,023 Sq. Ft.

TOTAL: 3,699 Sq. Ft.

BONUS ROOM: 487 Sq. Ft.

WIDTH: 87'-8" DEPTH: 63'-0"

COUNTRY ABUNDANCE

©1993 Donald A. Gardner Architects, Inc.

DESIGN FEATURES

BEDROOMS: 4

BATHROOMS: 3½

FIRST FLOOR: 2,357 Sq. Ft.

SECOND FLOOR: 995 Sq. Ft.

TOTAL: 3,352 Sq. Ft.

BONUS ROOM: 545 Sq. Ft.

WIDTH: 95'-4" DEPTH: 54'-10"

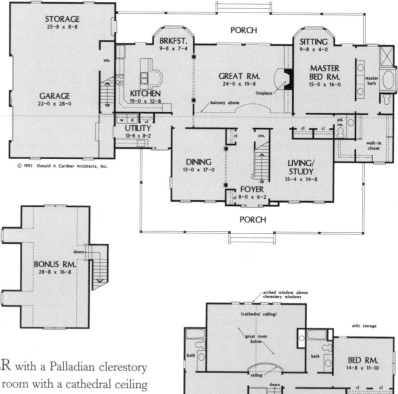

DESIGN HPT290090

DONALD A. GARDNER
ARCHITECTS, INC.

FROM THE TWO-STORY FOYER with a Palladian clerestory window and graceful stairway to the large great room with a cathedral ceiling and curved balcony, impressive spaces prevail in this open plan. A columned opening from the great room introduces the spacious family kitchen with a center island counter and breakfast bay. The master suite, privately located at the opposite end of the first floor, features a sitting bay, an extra-large walk-in closet and a bath with every possible luxury. Three bedrooms and two full baths make up the second floor, perfect for friends and family. A bonus room and attic storage offer expansion opportunities for the future.

THIS ROOMY COUNTRY HOME OFFERS a multitude of windows and two expansive porches. The foyer is flanked by the dining room on the left, and a bedroom (or optional study) on the right. The pantry offers ease of service with its placement between the kitchen and dining room. A bay window in the breakfast nook creates a sunny locale for casual dining. From the foyer, a view of the rear property draws you into the great room that features a fireplace, built-ins, a cathedral ceiling and an overlook from the second floor. The master suite is secluded on the right with access to the rear porch. The second floor boasts two bedrooms and a Jack and Jill bath.

DESIGN HPT290091

DONALD A. GARDNER
ARCHITECTS, INC.

DESIGN FEATURES

BEDROOMS: 4
BATHROOMS: 3½
FIRST FLOOR: 2,516 Sq. Ft.
SECOND FLOOR: 722 Sq. Ft.
TOTAL: 3,238 Sq. Ft.
BONUS ROOM: 513 Sq. Ft.
WIDTH: 72'-0" DEPTH: 60'-7"

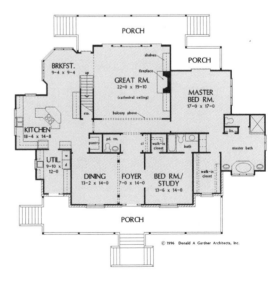

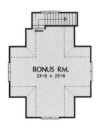

© 1993 Donald A. Gardner Architects, Inc.

DESIGN HPT290092

DONALD A. GARDNER
ARCHITECTS, INC.

THIS GRAND COUNTRY FARMHOUSE with a wraparound porch offers comfortable living at its finest. The open floor plan is accented by a vaulted great room and the entrance foyer with clerestory windows. The large kitchen provides lots of counter space, a sunny breakfast nook and a cooktop island with a bumped-out snack bar. The master suite has beautiful bay windows, a well-designed private bath and a spacious walk-in closet. The second level holds two large bedrooms, a full bath and plenty of attic storage.

DESIGN FEATURES

BEDROOMS: 4

BATHROOMS: 3½

FIRST FLOOR: 2,238 Sq. Ft.

SECOND FLOOR: 768 Sq. Ft.

TOTAL: 3,006 Sq. Ft.

WIDTH: 94'-1" DEPTH: 59'-10"

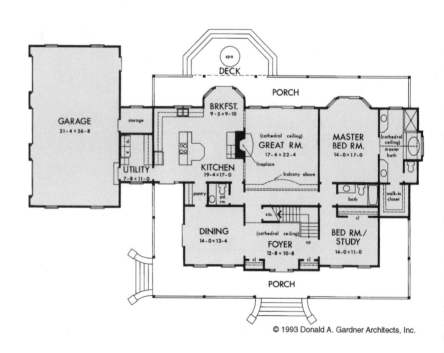

© 1993 Donald A. Gardner Architects, Inc.

©1993 Donald A. Gardner Architects, Inc.

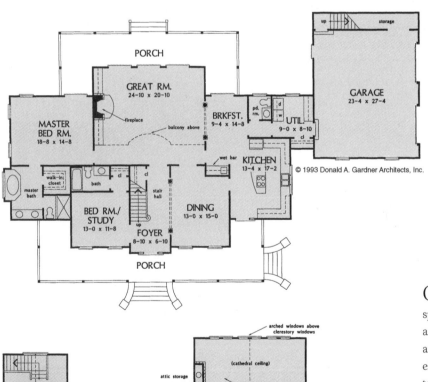

© 1993 Donald A. Gardner Architects, Inc.

DESIGN FEATURES

BEDROOMS: 5
BATHROOMS: 3½
FIRST FLOOR: 2,176 Sq. Ft.
SECOND FLOOR: 861 Sq. Ft.
TOTAL: 3,037 Sq. Ft.
BONUS ROOM: 483 Sq. Ft.
WIDTH: 94'-0" DEPTH: 58'-4"

DESIGN HPT290093

DONALD A. GARDNER
ARCHITECTS, INC.

COUNTRY LIVING is at its best in this spacious, five-bedroom farmhouse with a wrap-around porch. A front Palladian window dormer and rear clerestory windows add exciting visual elements to the exterior and provide natural light to the interior. The large great room boasts a fireplace, bookshelves and a raised cathedral ceiling, allowing the curved balcony to overlook from above. Special features such as a large cooktop island in the kitchen, a wet bar, a bedroom/study combination and a generous bonus room over the garage set this plan apart from the rest.

COUNTRY ABUNDANCE

© 1993 Donald A. Gardner Architects, Inc.

B·NATHAN·

C OUNTRY LIVING IS AT ITS BEST in this spacious four-bedroom farmhouse with a wraparound porch. A front Palladian window dormer and rear clerestory windows in the great room add exciting visual elements to the exterior, while providing natural light to the interior. In the great room, a fireplace, bookshelves, a cathedral ceiling and a balcony over-look create a comfortable atmosphere. The formal dining room is open to the foyer, while the living room could be used as a study instead. Special features such as a large cooktop island in the kitchen, a wet bar, a generous bonus room over the garage and ample storage space set this plan apart from oth-ers. You'll also love the fact that the master suite, the great room and the breakfast room all directly access the rear porch.

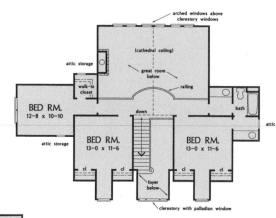

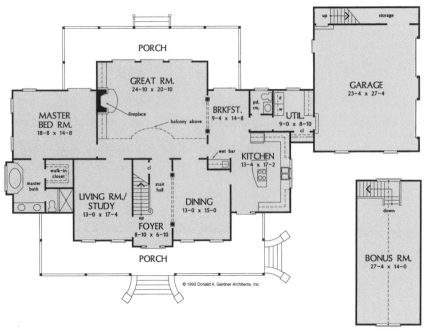

© 1993 Donald A. Gardner Architects, Inc.

DESIGN FEATURES

BEDROOMS: 4

BATHROOMS: 2½

FIRST FLOOR: 2,176 Sq. Ft.

SECOND FLOOR: 861 Sq. Ft.

TOTAL: 3,037 Sq. Ft.

BONUS ROOM: 483 Sq. Ft.

WIDTH: 94'-0" DEPTH: 58'-4"

DESIGN HPT290094

DONALD A. GARDNER
ARCHITECTS, INC.

DESIGN HPT290095

©BRELAND & FARMER
DESIGNERS, INC.

THIS STURDY BRICK and siding home begins with a lovely and inviting front porch. The entry leads into a family room with a thirteen-foot ceiling, fireplace and built-in entertainment center. Beyond the family room are the breakfast room and sun room, where a skylight and a bar with a wine rack, sink and glass shelves can be found. Packed full of amenities, the kitchen includes a pantry, built-in lazy Susans, a skylight and a bar. The master bedroom is a study in spaciousness with its large walk-in closet, sloped ceiling in the bathroom, skylight, linen closets, vanity and glass-surrounded spa tub. Bedrooms are just as lavish; one has a full bath, skylight and walk-in closet, while the other two have built-in desks and shelves, large closets and a mutual bath. Please specify crawlspace or slab foundation when ordering.

DESIGN FEATURES

BEDROOMS: 4
BATHROOMS: 3
TOTAL: 3,158 Sq. Ft.
WIDTH: 72'-0" DEPTH: 70'-0"

COUNTRY ABUNDANCE

DESIGN FEATURES

BEDROOMS: 4

BATHROOMS: 3½

FIRST FLOOR: 2,116 Sq. Ft.

SECOND FLOOR: 956 Sq. Ft.

TOTAL: 3,072 Sq. Ft.

WIDTH: 67'-8" DEPTH: 57'-0"

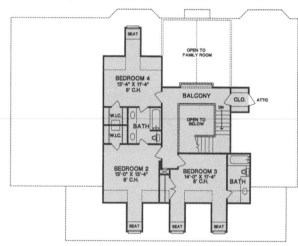

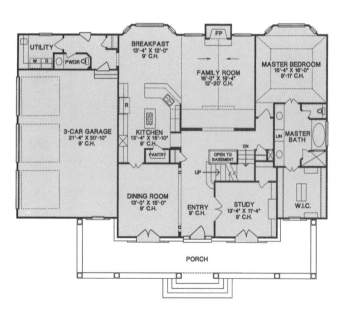

DESIGN HPT290096
©DESIGN BASICS, INC.

SYMMETRICAL SIMPLICITY incorporates balance and beauty in this luxurious country home. Artistic features throughout the plan provide unique style to every room. From the entry, columns elegantly frame the entrance to the formal dining room while two sets of double doors provide access—from both inside and out—to the study. To the rear of the plan, the family room enjoys a cathedral ceiling and natural light—also savored from the bay-windowed breakfast room and step-saving kitchen nearby. A tray ceiling adds a dramatic touch to the private master suite highlighted by a pampering bath. Each of the three family bedrooms upstairs has a dormer window seat and direct access to a full bath. Please specify basement, slab or block foundation when ordering.

DESIGN FEATURES

BEDROOMS: 4
BATHROOMS: 2½
FIRST FLOOR: 1,883 Sq. Ft.
SECOND FLOOR: 1,801 Sq. Ft.
TOTAL: 3,684 Sq. Ft.
WIDTH: 65'-4" DEPTH: 68'-0"

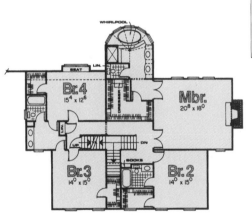

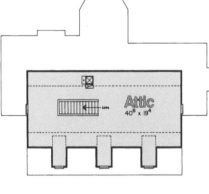

DESIGN HPT290097
©DESIGN BASICS, INC.

SHUTTERED MULTI-PANE WINDOWS and a wrap-around porch offer countryside comfort with this charming farmhouse design. A tiled entry opens to a traditional living room prepared for planned events, and to the formal dining room. An expansive kitchen has an island cooktop counter, double oven/microwave stack and a peninsula snack bar. The spacious breakfast area satisfies large and growing families, and provides wide outdoor views with a bay window. A cozy fireplace warms the family room, which has its own door to the porch. Upstairs, a grand master suite enjoys a luxurious private bath housed in a bay, with a whirlpool tub, a compartmented water closet and two lavatories. Two family bedrooms share a full bath that includes a compartmented vanity, while an additional bedroom has its own bath.

DESIGN HPT290098

DONALD A. GARDNER
ARCHITECTS, INC.

FILLED WITH THE CHARM of farmhouse details, this design opens with a classic covered porch at the front. The entry leads to a foyer flanked by columns that separate the formal dining room on the right from the formal living room on the left. Straight ahead, decorated by another column, the family room boasts a two-story ceiling, a fireplace and sliding glass doors to the rear covered porch. The U-shaped kitchen separates the dining room from the bayed breakfast room. The first-floor master suite features a bedroom with a tray ceiling and a bath with a whirlpool tub, dual sinks and a separate shower. Two walk-in closets complete the suite. Two family bedrooms on the second floor are joined by a loft overlooking the family room.

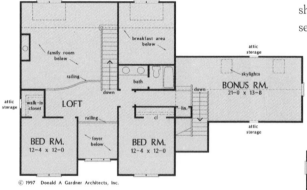

DESIGN FEATURES

BEDROOMS: 3

BATHROOMS: 2

FIRST FLOOR: 1,914 Sq. Ft.

SECOND FLOOR: 597 Sq. Ft.

TOTAL: 2,511 Sq. Ft.

BONUS ROOM: 487 Sq. Ft.

WIDTH: 79'-2" DEPTH: 51'-6"

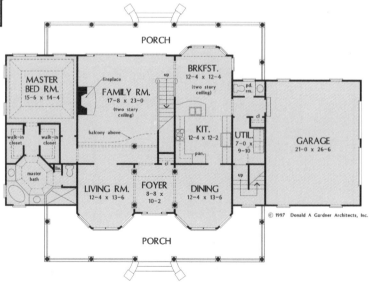

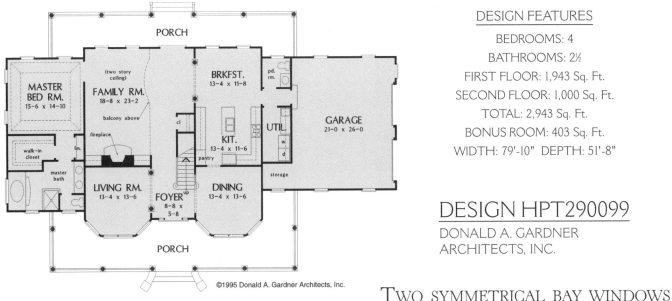

PORCH

MASTER
BED RM.
15-6 x 14-10

walk-in
closet

master
bath

lin.

(two story
ceiling)

FAMILY RM.
18-8 x 23-2

balcony above

fireplace

LIVING RM.
13-4 x 13-6

FOYER
8-8 x
5-8

cl

BRKFST.
13-4 x 11-8

pd.
rm.

KIT.
13-4 x 11-6

pantry

DINING
13-4 x 13-6

UTIL.

w
d

storage

GARAGE
21-0 x 26-0

PORCH

©1995 Donald A. Gardner Architects, Inc.

family room
below

LOFT/
STUDY
8-8 x 9-10

railing

cl

cl

down

BED RM.
13-4 x 13-6

walk-in
closet

BED RM.
13-4 x 11-10

attic storage

lin.

cl

skylights

BONUS RM.
27-0 x 14-0

bath

attic storage

BED RM.
13-4 x 13-6

© 1995 Donald A Gardner Architects, Inc.

DESIGN FEATURES

BEDROOMS: 4
BATHROOMS: 2½
FIRST FLOOR: 1,943 Sq. Ft.
SECOND FLOOR: 1,000 Sq. Ft.
TOTAL: 2,943 Sq. Ft.
BONUS ROOM: 403 Sq. Ft.
WIDTH: 79'-10" DEPTH: 51'-8"

DESIGN HPT290099

DONALD A. GARDNER
ARCHITECTS, INC.

TWO SYMMETRICAL BAY WINDOWS
accent the formal living room and dining room of this
design. The foyer leads straight back to the family room and
rear porch. A fireplace, built-ins and an overhead balcony
grace the family room. Between the dining room and
kitchen, there's a handy pantry area. The utility room and a
powder room are to the right of the breakfast room. The
master suite sits just off the family room and includes a
walk-in closet and a bath with a double-bowl vanity.
Upstairs, three bedrooms share a hall bath and a loft/study
that overlooks the family room.

COUNTRY ABUNDANCE

DESIGN HPT290100

©DESIGN BASICS, INC.

ON THE SMALL SIDE, BUT FILLED with amenities, this fine four-bedroom home is a pleasant surprise. Inside, surprises include a kitchen with snack bar, master bathroom with separate dressing area and soaking tub, and a cathedral-ceilinged family room with transom windows and fireplace. The foyer opens to the family room and the dining room conveniently situated near the kitchen and breakfast nook that overlooks the backyard. Three family bedrooms share two full baths on the second floor while the master suite finds privacy on the first floor.

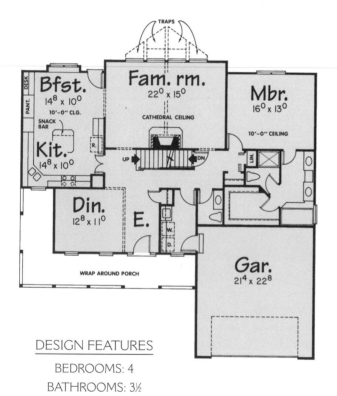

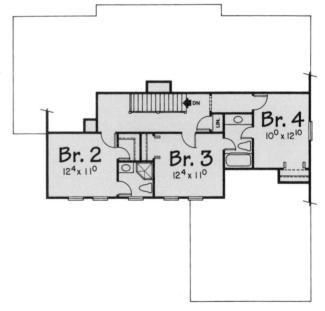

DESIGN FEATURES

BEDROOMS: 4

BATHROOMS: 3½

FIRST FLOOR: 1,597 Sq. Ft.

SECOND FLOOR: 735 Sq. Ft.

TOTAL: 2,332 Sq. Ft.

WIDTH: 54'-0"   DEPTH: 52'-0"

Quote One®
Cost to build? See page 186
to order complete cost estimate
to build this house in your area!

DESIGN HPT290101
©STEPHEN FULLER, INC.

THE COVERED FRONT STOOP of this two-story traditionally styled home gives way to the foyer and formal areas inside. A cozy living room with a fireplace sits on the right and an elongated dining room is on the left. For fine family living, a great room and a kitchen/breakfast area account for the rear of the first-floor plan. A guest room with a nearby full bath finishes off the accommodations. Upstairs, four bedrooms include a master suite fit for royalty. A bonus room rests near Bedroom 3 and would make a great office or additional bedroom. This home is designed with a walkout basement foundation.

DESIGN FEATURES

BEDROOMS: 5
BATHROOMS: 4
FIRST FLOOR: 1,700 Sq. Ft.
SECOND FLOOR: 1,585 Sq. Ft.
TOTAL: 3,285 Sq. Ft.
BONUS ROOM: 176 Sq. Ft.
WIDTH: 60'-0" DEPTH: 47'-6"

DESIGN HPT290102

©STEPHEN FULLER, INC.

DESIGN FEATURES

BEDROOMS: 4

BATHROOMS: 3½

FIRST FLOOR: 1,475 Sq. Ft.

SECOND FLOOR: 1,460 Sq. Ft.

TOTAL: 2,935 Sq. Ft.

WIDTH: 57'-6" DEPTH: 46'-6"

QUAINT KEYSTONES AND SHUTTERS offer charming accents to the stucco-and-stone exterior of this stately English country home. The two-story foyer opens through decorative columns to the formal living room, which offers a wet bar. The nearby media room shares a through-fireplace with the two-story great room, which has double doors that lead to the rear deck. A bumped-out bay holds a breakfast area that shares its light with an expansive cooktop-island kitchen. This area opens to the formal dining room through a convenient butler's pantry. One wing of the second floor is dedicated to the rambling master suite, which boasts unusual amenities: the bedroom features angled walls, a tray ceiling and a bumped-out bay with a sitting area. This home is designed with a walkout basement foundation.

Quote One®

Cost to build? See page 186
to order complete cost estimate
to build this house in your area!

DECK

BREAKFAST
10'-0" X 13'-0"

FAMILY ROOM
17'-6" X 17'-6"

PANTRY

KITCHEN
17'-2" X 15'-6"

STORAGE

LAUNDRY

DN.

POWDER

WET BAR

TWO CAR GARAGE
21'-0" X 21'-6"

DINING ROOM
13'-0" X 14'-6"

UP

FOYER
11'-0" X 15'-4"

LIVING ROOM
12'-10" X 12'-0"

PORCH

DESIGN FEATURES

BEDROOMS: 4

BATHROOMS: 3½

FIRST FLOOR: 1,570 Sq. Ft.

SECOND FLOOR: 1,630 Sq. Ft.

TOTAL: 3,200 Sq. Ft.

WIDTH: 59'-10"   DEPTH: 43'-4"

DESIGN HPT290103
©STEPHEN FULLER, INC.

THIS CLASSIC AMERICANA design employs wood siding, a variety of window styles and a detailed front porch. Inside, the large two-story foyer flows into the formal dining room with arched window accents and the living room highlighted by a bay window. A short passage with a wet bar accesses the family room with its wall of windows, French doors and fireplace. The large breakfast area and open island kitchen are spacious and airy as well as efficient. Upstairs, the master suite's sleeping and sitting rooms feature architectural details including columns, tray ceilings and a fireplace. The elegant private bath contains a raised oval tub, dual vanities and a separate shower. A generous walk-in closet is located beyond the bath. Additional bedrooms are complete with closets and a variety of bath combinations. This home is designed with a walkout basement foundation.

W.I.C.

BEDROOM NO. 2
13'-8" X 11'-0"

MASTER BEDROOM
15'-4" X 13'-0"

SITTING ROOM
12'-0" X 13'-0"

BATH

BEDROOM NO. 4
11'-10" X 14'-0"

BATH

DN.

MASTER BATH

W.I.C.

BEDROOM NO. 3
13'-0" X 12'-2"

OPEN TO BELOW

W.I.C.

UNFIN. STORAGE
10'-4" X 11'-6"

A SYMMETRICAL FACADE with twin chimneys makes a grand statement on this home. A covered porch welcomes visitors and provides a pleasant place to spend a mild evening. The entry foyer is flanked by formal living areas: a dining room and a living room, each with a fireplace. A third fireplace is the highlight of the expansive great room to the rear. An L-shaped kitchen offers a work island and a walk-in pantry as amenities and easily serves the nearby breakfast and sun rooms. The deck is accessible through the great room, the sun room or the master bedroom. The first-floor master suite is lavish in its luxuries: His and Hers walk-in closets, a sunny bay window and a sumptuous bath. The second floor offers three bedrooms, two full baths and plenty of storage space. This home is designed with a walkout basement foundation.

QUOTE ONE®

Cost to build? See page 186 to order complete cost estimate to build this house in your area!

DESIGN HPT290104
©STEPHEN FULLER, INC.

DESIGN FEATURES

BEDROOMS: 3
BATHROOMS: 3½
FIRST FLOOR: 2,565 Sq. Ft.
SECOND FLOOR: 1,375 Sq. Ft.
TOTAL: 3,940 Sq. Ft.
WIDTH: 88'-6" DEPTH: 50'-10"

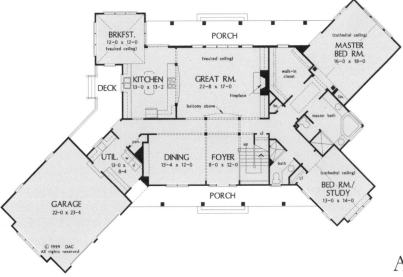

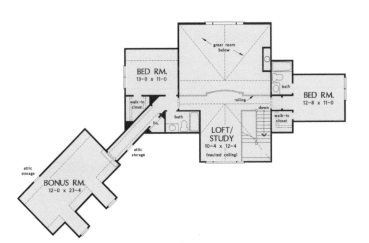

DESIGN FEATURES

BEDROOMS: 4

BATHROOMS: 4

FIRST FLOOR: 2,477 Sq. Ft.

SECOND FLOOR: 819 Sq. Ft.

TOTAL: 3,296 Sq. Ft.

BONUS ROOM: 360 Sq. Ft.

WIDTH: 100'-0" DEPTH: 66'-2"

DESIGN HPT290105

DONALD A. GARDNER
ARCHITECTS, INC.

A PROMINENT CENTER GABLE with an arched window accents the facade of this custom Craftsman home, which features an exterior of cedar shakes, siding and stone. An open floor plan with generously proportioned rooms contributes to the home's spacious and relaxed atmosphere. The vaulted great room boasts a rear wall of windows, a fireplace bordered by built-in cabinets, and convenient access to the kitchen. A second-floor loft overlooks the great room for added drama. The master suite is completely secluded and enjoys a cathedral ceiling, back-porch access, a large walk-in closet and a luxurious bath. The home includes three additional bedrooms and baths as well as a vaulted loft/study and bonus room.

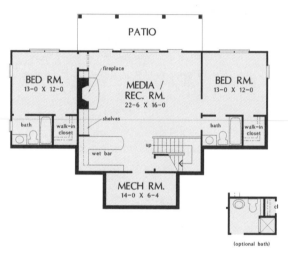

DESIGN HPT290106

DONALD A. GARDNER
ARCHITECTS, INC.

STONE, SIDING AND MULTIPLE GABLES combine beautifully on the exterior of this hillside home. Taking advantage of rear views, the home's most oft-used rooms are oriented at the back with plenty of windows. Augmented by a cathedral ceiling, the great room features a fireplace, built-in shelves and access to the rear deck. Twin walk-in closets and a private bath infuse the master suite with luxury. The nearby powder room offers an optional full-bath arrangement, allowing the study to double as a bedroom. Downstairs, a large media/recreation room with a wet bar and fireplace separates two more bedrooms, each with a full bath and walk-in closet.

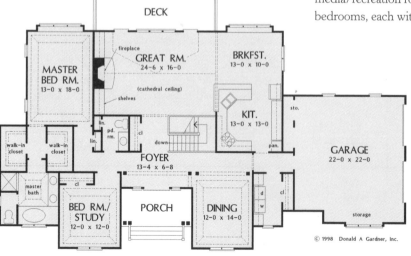

© 1998 Donald A Gardner, Inc.

DESIGN FEATURES

BEDROOMS: 4

BATHROOMS: 3½

MAIN LEVEL: 2,065 Sq. Ft.

FINISHED BASEMENT: 1,216 Sq. Ft.

TOTAL: 3,281 Sq. Ft.

WIDTH: 82'-2" DEPTH: 43'-6"

© 1999 Donald A. Gardner

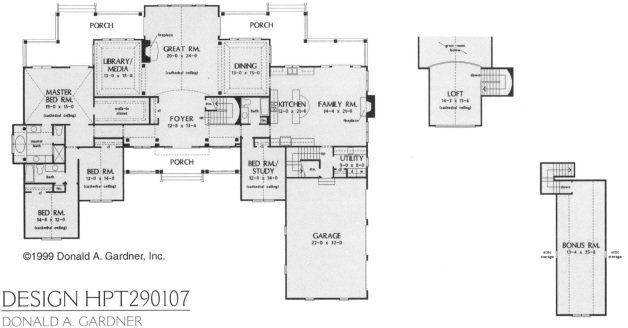

©1999 Donald A. Gardner, Inc.

DESIGN HPT290107

DONALD A. GARDNER
ARCHITECTS, INC.

THIS EXTRAORDINARY FOUR-BEDROOM estate features gables with decorative wood brackets, arched windows and a stone and siding facade for undeniable Craftsman character. At the heart of the home, a magnificent cathedral ceiling adds space and stature to the impressive great room, which accesses both back porches. Sharing the great room's cathedral ceiling, the loft makes an excellent reading nook. Tray ceilings adorn the dining room and library/media room, while all four bedrooms enjoy cathedral ceilings. A sizeable kitchen is open to a large gathering room for ultimate family togetherness. The master suite features back-porch access, a lavish private bath and an oversized walk-in closet. A spacious bonus room is located over the three-car garage for further expansion.

DESIGN FEATURES

BEDROOMS: 4
BATHROOMS: 3
FIRST FLOOR: 3,555 Sq. Ft.
SECOND FLOOR: 250 Sq. Ft.
TOTAL: 3,805 Sq. Ft.
BONUS ROOM: 490 Sq. Ft.
WIDTH: 99'-8" DEPTH: 78'-8"

117

DESIGN FEATURES

BEDROOMS: 4

BATHROOMS: 3½

FIRST FLOOR: 2,076 Sq. Ft.

SECOND FLOOR: 843 Sq. Ft.

TOTAL: 2,919 Sq. Ft.

WIDTH: 57'-6"   DEPTH: 51'-6"

DESIGN HPT290108

©STEPHEN FULLER, INC.

THIS LOVELY HOME'S FOYER opens to the formal dining room, defined by decorative columns, and leads to the two-story great room. The kitchen and breakfast room join the great room to create a casual family area. The master suite is finished with a coffered ceiling and a sumptuous bath. A guest suite with a private bath is located just off the kitchen. Upstairs two family bedrooms share a compartmented bath and a raised loft. This home is designed with a walkout basement foundation.

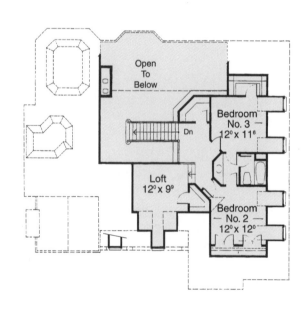

IF YOU WISH TO LIVE IN THE DESERT SOUTHWEST

or on the coast of California or Florida, there are special styles of

architecture that will enhance your relaxed, sun-loving lifestyle for

years to come. Take for instance the Pueblo style, with its distinctive

thick adobe walls, flat rooflines, projecting wood beams called vigas

and long covered porches. Or the Mission-style home, with its

attractive tile roof and broad porches. If the tropical scene is more

to your liking, homes with stucco walls and low-pitched rooflines

will meet your needs nicely. All styles also feature open, spacious

rooms. Whatever you desire, there is a style to help you in your

search for the sun.

SHOWN ABOVE:

DESIGN HPT290113

BY HOME PLANNERS.

SEE PAGE 124 FOR

MORE INFORMATION

ON THIS ATTRACTIVE

SANTA FE HOME.

DESIGN HPT290109
©HOME PLANNERS

DESIGN FEATURES

BEDROOMS: 4

BATHROOMS: 3

TOTAL: 3,144 Sq. Ft.

WIDTH: 139'-10" DEPTH: 63'-8"

L

IN CLASSIC SOUTHWESTERN STYLE, this home strikes a beautiful balance between preserving the historic integrity of its classic style and the open spirit of a contemporary interior. A covered porch runs the width of the front exterior and extends the living areas to the outdoors. A rambling family kitchen invites casual gatherings and lively conversations. To the right of the plan, family bedrooms share a full bath and look out to the rear property and terrace. The master suite—complete with its own fireplace—enjoys privacy nestled in a quiet wing it shares with a study, which could double as a guest room. The private bath offers a corner whirlpool tub, twin vanity sinks and a shower.

QUOTE ONE®

Cost to build? See page 186
to order complete cost estimate
to build this house in your area!

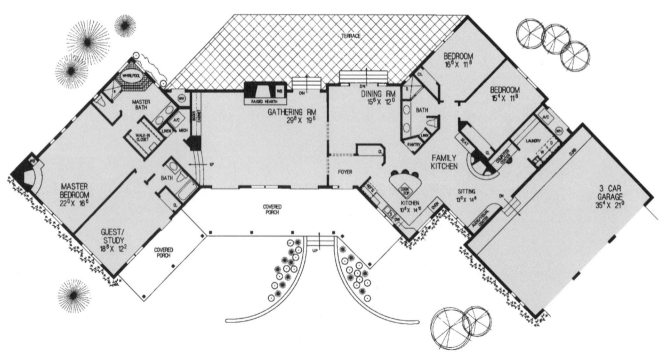

AN IN-LINE FLOOR PLAN follows the tradition of the original Santa Fe-style homes. The slight curve to the overall configuration lends an interesting touch. From the front courtyard, the plan opens to a formal living room and dining room, complemented by a family room and a kitchen with an adjoining morning room. The master suite is found to one side of the plan while family bedrooms share space at the opposite end. There's also a huge office and a bonus/study area for private times.

DESIGN FEATURES

BEDROOMS: 4
BATHROOMS: 3½
TOTAL: 3,428 Sq. Ft.
WIDTH: 120'-0" DEPTH: 86'-0"

L

DESIGN HPT290110
©HOME PLANNERS

Quote One®

Cost to build? See page 186
to order complete cost estimate
to build this house in your area!

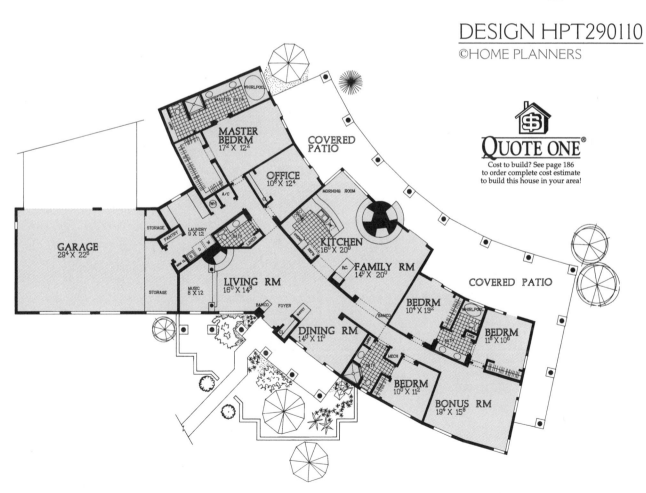

DESIGN HPT290111
©HOME PLANNERS

THIS DIAMOND IN THE DESERT gives new meaning to old style. A courtyard leads to a covered porch with nooks for sitting and open-air dining. The gracious living room is highlighted by a corner fireplace, while the formal dining room comes with an adjacent butler's pantry and access to the porch dining area. Two sleeping zones are luxurious with whirlpool tubs and separate showers. The master suite also boasts an exercise room and a nearby private office. A guest suite includes a private entrance and another corner fireplace.

QUOTE ONE®
Cost to build? See page 186
to order complete cost estimate
to build this house in your area!

DESIGN FEATURES

BEDROOMS: 4

BATHROOMS: 2½ + ½

TOTAL: 3,838 Sq. Ft.

WIDTH: 126'-7" DEPTH: 60'-10"

THE IMPRESSIVE, DOUBLE-DOOR ENTRY to the walled court-
yard sets the tone for this Santa Fe masterpiece home. The expansive great room shows
off its casual style with a centerpiece fireplace and abundant windows overlooking the
patio. Joining the great room is the formal dining room, again graced with windows and
patio doors. The large gourmet kitchen has an eat-in snack bar and joins the family
room to create a warm atmosphere for casual entertaining. Family-room extras include
a fireplace, entertainment built-ins and double doors to the front courtyard. Just off the
family room are the two large family bedrooms, which share a private bath. The relaxing master suite is located off the great room and has double doors to the back patio.

DESIGN HPT290112
©HOME PLANNERS

Quote One®
Cost to build? See page 186
to order complete cost estimate
to build this house in your area!

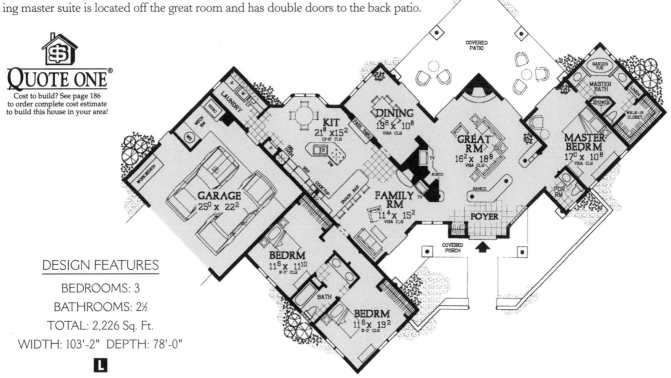

DESIGN FEATURES

BEDROOMS: 3
BATHROOMS: 2½
TOTAL: 2,226 Sq. Ft.
WIDTH: 103'-2" DEPTH: 78'-0"

L

STUNNING SUN COUNTRY

DESIGN FEATURES

BEDROOMS: 3

BATHROOMS: 2½

TOTAL: 2,350 Sq. Ft.

WIDTH: 92'-7" DEPTH: 79'-0"

L

QUOTE ONE®

Cost to build? See page 186
to order complete cost estimate
to build this house in your area!

DESIGN HPT290113
©HOME PLANNERS

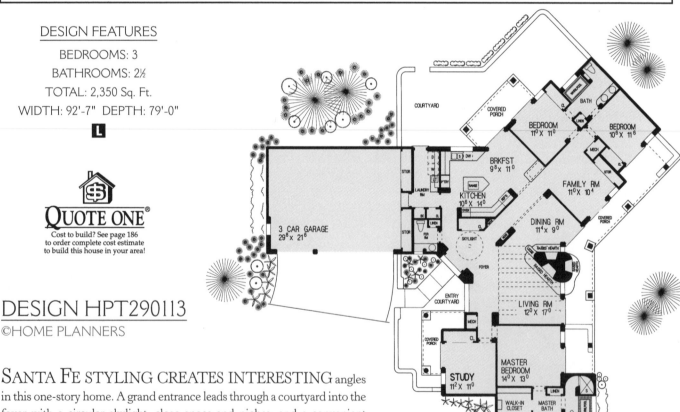

SANTA FE STYLING CREATES INTERESTING angles in this one-story home. A grand entrance leads through a courtyard into the foyer with a circular skylight, close space and niches, and a convenient powder room. Turn right to the master suite with a deluxe bath and a bedroom close at hand, perfect for a nursery, home office or exercise room. Two more family bedrooms are placed quietly in the far wing of the house. Make note of the island cooktop in the kitchen, the extra storage in the garage and the covered porches on two sides.

HERE'S A RAMBLING RANCH with a unique configuration. Massive double doors at the front entrance are sheltered by the covered porch. This well-zoned plan offers exceptional one-story livability for the active family. The central foyer routes traffic effectively while featuring a feeling of spaciousness. Note the dramatic columns that accentuate the big living room with its high 17'-8" ceiling. This interesting, angular room has a commanding corner fireplace with a raised hearth, a wall of windows, a doorway to the huge rear covered porch and a pass-through to the kitchen. The informal family room directly accesses the rear porch and is handy to the three children's bedrooms. At the opposite end of the plan, and guaranteed its full measure of privacy, is the large master suite. The master bedroom, with its high ceiling, enjoys direct access to the rear porch.

Quote One®
Cost to build? See page 186
to order complete cost estimate
to build this house in your area!

DESIGN HPT290114
©HOME PLANNERS

DESIGN FEATURES

BEDROOMS: 4

BATHROOMS: 3½

TOTAL: 2,966 Sq. Ft.

WIDTH: 116'-7" DEPTH: 77'-5"

L

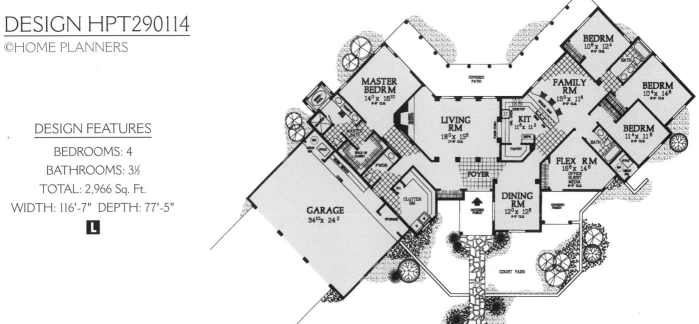

DESIGN HPT290115
©HOME PLANNERS

UNIQUE IN NATURE, this two-story Santa Fe-style home is as practical as it is lovely. The entry foyer leads past a curving staircase to living areas at the back of the plan. These include a living room with a corner fireplace and a family room connected to the kitchen via a built-in eating nook. The kitchen furthers its appeal with an island cooktop and a snack bar. Two family bedrooms on this level include one with a private covered patio. They share a full bath that includes dual lavatories and a whirlpool tub. Upstairs, the master suite features a grand bath, corner fireplace, large walk-in closet and private balcony. A guest bedroom accesses a full bath. Every room in this home has its own outdoor area.

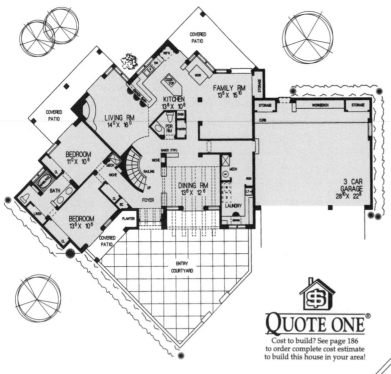

QUOTE ONE®
Cost to build? See page 186
to order complete cost estimate
to build this house in your area!

DESIGN FEATURES

BEDROOMS: 4
BATHROOMS: 3½
FIRST FLOOR: 1,966 Sq. Ft.
SECOND FLOOR: 831 Sq. Ft.
TOTAL: 2,797 Sq. Ft.
WIDTH: 90'-0" DEPTH: 51'-8"

L

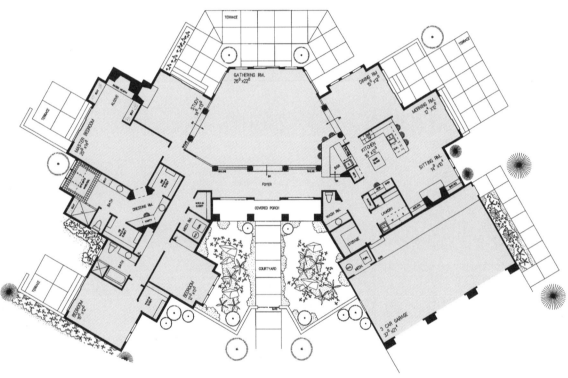

DESIGN HPT290116
©HOME PLANNERS

LOADED WITH CUSTOM FEATURES, this plan is designed to delight the imagination. The foyer enters directly into the commanding sunken gathering room. Framed by an elegant railing, this centerpiece for entertaining opens to both the study and the formal dining room, and provides sliding glass doors to the terrace. A full bar further extends the entertaining possibilities of this room. The country-style kitchen contains an efficient work area, as well as a morning room and sitting area that's ideal for family gatherings around the cozy fireplace. The grand master suite showcases a private terrace, a fireplace alcove with built-in seats and a huge spa-style bath. Two nicely sized bedrooms and a hall bath round out the plan.

DESIGN FEATURES
BEDROOMS: 3
BATHROOMS: 2½
TOTAL: 3,505 Sq. Ft.
WIDTH: 110'-7" DEPTH: 66'-11"

INNOVATIVE DESIGN and attention to detail create true luxury living. This clean, contemporary-style home features a raised, columned entry with an interesting stucco relief archway. The foyer opens to the formal living room, which overlooks the lanai and waterfall through walls of glass. The formal dining room has a curved wall of windows and a built-in buffet table. Two guest suites each boast a walk-in closet and a private bath. The master suite features a foyer with views of a fountain and a sunny sitting area that opens to the lanai. The bath beckons with a soaking tub, round shower and large wardrobe area.

DESIGN HPT290117

©THE SATER DESIGN COLLECTION

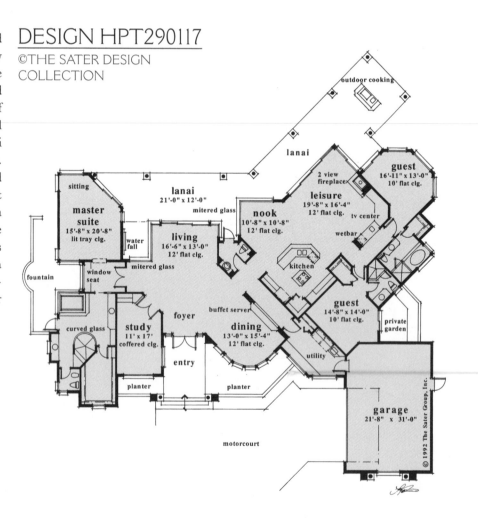

DESIGN FEATURES

BEDROOMS: 3
BATHROOMS: 3½
TOTAL: 3,944 Sq. Ft.
WIDTH: 98'-0" DEPTH: 105'-0"

L

DESIGN HPT290118

©THE SATER DESIGN
COLLECTION

THIS MODERN HOME ADDS a contemporary twist to the typical ranch-style plan. The turret study and bayed dining room add a sensuous look from the streetscape. The main living areas open up to the lanai and offer broad views to the rear through large expanses of glass and doors. The family kitchen, nook and leisure room focus on the lanai, the entertainment center and an ale bar. The guest suites have separate baths and also access the lanai. The master bath features a curved-glass shower, whirlpool tub, and private toilet and bidet room. Dual walk-in closets and an abundance of light further the appeal of this suite.

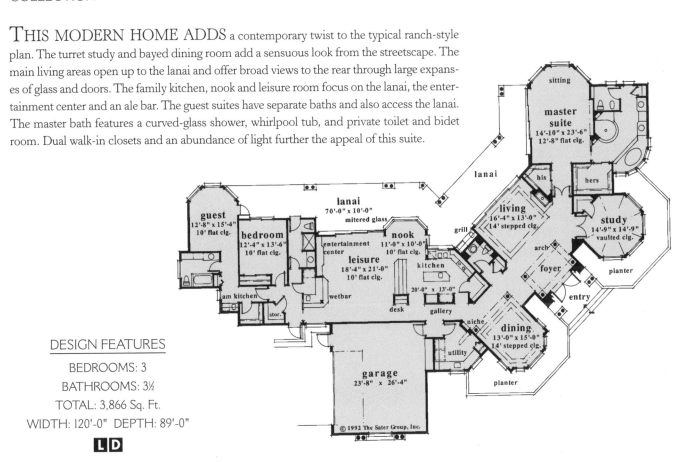

DESIGN FEATURES

BEDROOMS: 3

BATHROOMS: 3½

TOTAL: 3,866 Sq. Ft.

WIDTH: 120'-0"   DEPTH: 89'-0"

L D

DESIGN HPT290119
©THE SATER DESIGN
COLLECTION

IF SPACIOUS, CONTEMPORARY
living is your style, this grand design may suit you
perfectly. With gardens on either side, the barrel-
ceilinged entry sets the tone for a great interior. The
gourmet kitchen opens up with an island cooktop
and an abundance of storage space. Nearby, two
bedrooms share a full bath. An archway on the left
side of the plan leads to the master bedroom suite.
His and Hers closets and a lavish bath overlooking
a private garden define this room. A study with
plenty of built-ins and a full bath with outside
access complete the plan.

DESIGN FEATURES

BEDROOMS: 3
BATHROOMS: 3
TOTAL: 3,324 Sq. Ft.
WIDTH: 74'-0" DEPTH: 89'-8"

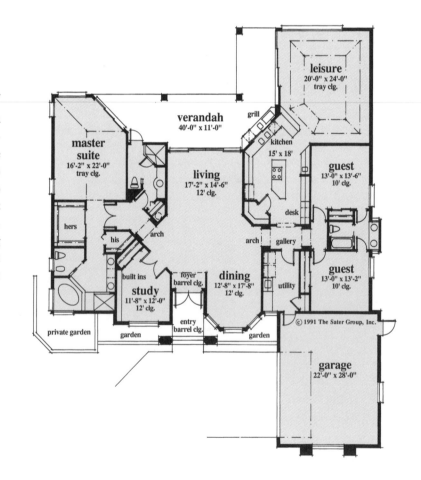

THIS FLORIDA CONTEMPORARY home is a best seller among families who insist on formal and casual living spaces. The master retreat, with a bay sitting area, is secluded away from the family area for quiet and solitude. The master bath includes a sumptuous soaking tub, shower for two, His and Hers vanities and a huge walk-in closet. The secondary bedrooms share a split bath, designed for dual use as well as privacy. The kitchen, nook and family room all provide magnificent views of the outdoor living space. Note the media wall in the family area—a must for today's sophisticated buyers.

DESIGN HPT290120

©HOME DESIGN
SERVICES, INC.

DESIGN FEATURES

BEDROOMS: 3

BATHROOMS: 3

TOTAL: 2,480 Sq. Ft.

WIDTH: 67'-4" DEPTH: 70'-8"

DESIGN HPT290121
©THE SATER DESIGN
COLLECTION

MAKE DREAMS COME TRUE
with this fine sunny design. An octagonal study
provides a nice focal point both inside and outside. The living areas remain open to each other
and access outdoor areas. A wet bar makes
entertaining a breeze, especially with a window
pass-through to a grill area on the lanai. The
kitchen enjoys shared space with a lovely breakfast nook and a bright leisure room. Two bedrooms are located near the family living center.
In the master bedroom suite, luxury abounds
with a two-way fireplace, a morning kitchen, two
walk-in closets and a compartmented bath.
Another full bath accommodates a pool area.

QUOTE ONE®
Cost to build? See page 186
to order complete cost estimate
to build this house in your area!

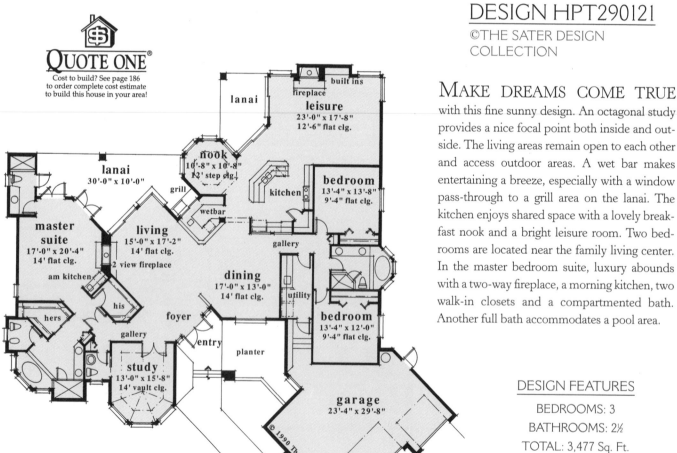

DESIGN FEATURES
BEDROOMS: 3
BATHROOMS: 2½
TOTAL: 3,477 Sq. Ft.
WIDTH: 95'-0" DEPTH: 88'-8"

DESIGN HPT290122

©THE SATER DESIGN
COLLECTION

THIS ELEGANT EXTERIOR blends a classical look with a contemporary feel. Corner quoins and round columns highlight the front elevation. The formal living room, complete with a fireplace and a wet bar, and the formal dining room access the lanai through three pairs of French doors. The well-appointed kitchen features an island prep sink, a walk-in pantry and a desk. The secondary bedrooms are full guest suites, located away from the master suite. This suite enjoys enormous His and Hers closets, built-ins, a wet bar and a three-sided fireplace that separates the sitting room and the bedroom. The luxurious bath features a stunning, rounded glass-block shower and a whirlpool tub.

DESIGN FEATURES

BEDROOMS: 3

BATHROOMS: 4½ + ½

TOTAL: 3,896 Sq. Ft.

BONUS ROOM: 356 Sq. Ft.

WIDTH: 90'-0" DEPTH: 120'-8"

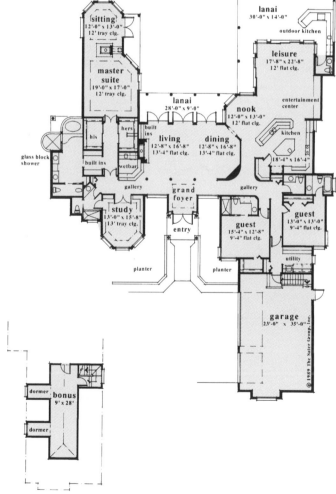

BRINGING THE OUTDOORS IN through a multitude of bay windows is what this design is all about. The grand foyer opens to the living room with a magnificent view to the covered lanai. The study and dining room flank the foyer. The master suite is found on the left with an opulent private bath and views of the private garden. To the right, the kitchen adjoins the nook that boasts a mitered glass bay window overlooking the lanai. Beyond the leisure room are two guest rooms, each with a private bath.

DESIGN FEATURES

BEDROOMS: 3
BATHROOMS: 3½
TOTAL: 3,398 Sq. Ft.
WIDTH: 121'-5" DEPTH: 96'-2"

DESIGN HPT290123

©THE SATER DESIGN
COLLECTION

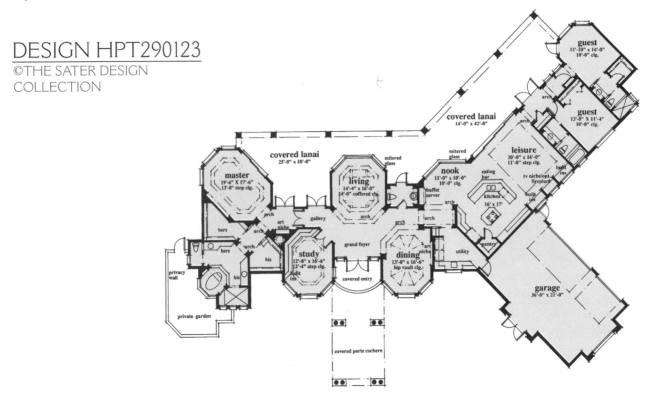

DESIGN FEATURES

BEDROOMS: 3
BATHROOMS: 3
TOTAL: 2,987 Sq. Ft.
WIDTH: 74'-4" DEPTH: 82'-4"

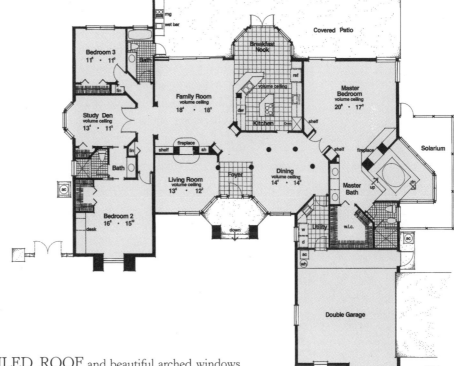

DESIGN HPT290124

©HOME DESIGN
SERVICES, INC.

CLASSIC COLUMNS, A TILED ROOF and beautiful arched windows herald a gracious interior for this fine home. Arched windows also mark the entrance into the vaulted living room with a tiled fireplace. The dining room opens off the vaulted foyer. Filled with light from a wall of sliding glass doors, the family room leads to the covered patio—note the wet bar and range that enhance outdoor living. The kitchen features a vaulted ceiling and unfolds into the roomy nook which boasts French doors to the patio. The master bedroom also has patio access and shares a dual fireplace with the master bath. A solarium lights this space. A vaulted study/bedroom sits between two additional bedrooms—all share a full bath.

DESIGN FEATURES

BEDROOMS: 4

BATHROOMS: 3½

FIRST FLOOR: 2,853 Sq. Ft.

SECOND FLOOR: 627 Sq. Ft.

TOTAL: 3,480 Sq. Ft.

GUEST HOUSE: 312 Sq. Ft.

WIDTH: 80'-0" DEPTH: 96'-0"

A UNIQUE COURTYARD PROVIDES a happy marriage of indoor/outdoor relationships for this design. Inside, the foyer opens to a grand salon with a wall of glass, providing unobstructed views of the backyard. Informal areas include a leisure room with an entertainment center and glass doors that open to a covered poolside lanai. An outdoor fireplace enhances casual gatherings. The master suite is filled with amenities that include a bayed sitting area, access to the rear lanai, His and Hers closets and a soaking tub. Upstairs, two family bedrooms—both with private decks—share a full bath. A detached guest house has a cabana bath and an outdoor grill area.

DESIGN HPT290125
©THE SATER DESIGN
COLLECTION

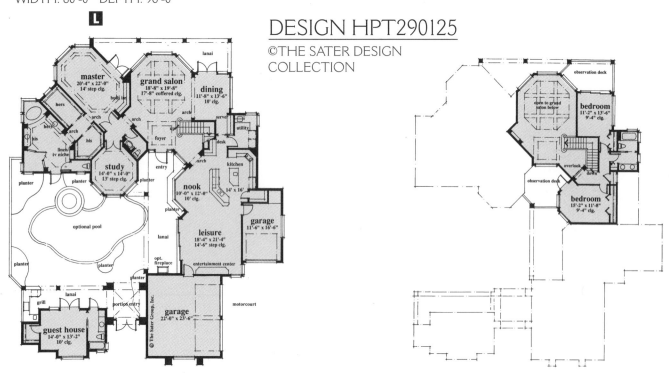

DESIGN HPT290126

©HOME DESIGN
SERVICES, INC.

THIS ONE-STORY HOME sports
many well-chosen, distinctive exterior details,
including a cameo window and hipped
rooflines. The dining and living rooms flank
the foyer. A tray ceiling in the living room adds
further enhancement. The bayed breakfast
area admits light softened by the patio.
Secluded from the main portion of the house,
the master bedroom features a tray ceiling and
a fireplace through to the private bath. A raised
tub, double vanity and immense walk-in closet
highlight the bath. Three family bedrooms line
the opposite end of the plan.

DESIGN FEATURES

BEDROOMS: 4
BATHROOMS: 3
TOTAL: 2,454 Sq. Ft.
WIDTH: 66'-8" DEPTH: 56'-8"

DESIGN HPT290127

©THE SATER DESIGN
COLLECTION

IN THE DELUXE GRAND ROOM of this Floridian home, family and friends will enjoy the ambiance created by arches and access to a veranda. Two guest rooms flank a full bath—one of the guest rooms also sports a private deck. The kitchen serves a circular breakfast nook. Upstairs, a balcony overlook furthers the drama of the grand room. The master suite, with a deck and a private bath opening through a pocket door, will be a pleasure to occupy. Another bedroom—or use this room for a study—sits at the other side of this floor. It extends a curved bay window, an expansive deck, built-ins and a full bath. The lower level contains enough room for two cars in its carport and offers plenty of storage and bonus room.

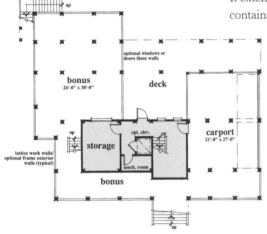

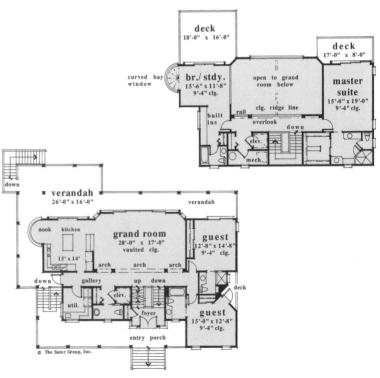

DESIGN FEATURES

BEDROOMS: 4

BATHROOMS: 4½

FIRST FLOOR: 1,944 Sq. Ft.

SECOND FLOOR: 1,196 Sq. Ft.

TOTAL: 3,335 Sq. Ft.

WIDTH: 68'-0" DEPTH: 54'-0"

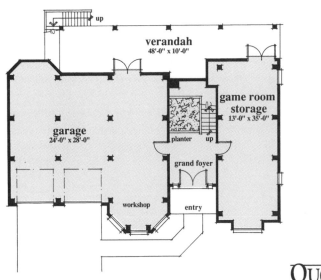

verandah
48'-0" x 10'-0"

game room
storage
13'-0" x 35'-0"

garage
24'-0" x 28'-0"

planter up

grand foyer

workshop

entry

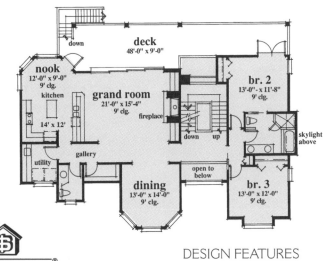

deck
48'-0" x 9'-0"

down

nook
12'-0" x 9'-0"
9' clg.

kitchen

14' x 12'

grand room
21'-0" x 15'-4"
9' clg.

fireplace

br. 2
13'-0" x 11'-8"
9' clg.

down up

skylight
above

utility

gallery

open to
below

dining
13'-0" x 14'-0"
9' clg.

br. 3
13'-0" x 12'-0"
9' clg.

deck
28'-0" x 8'-0"

2 view fireplace

master
suite
22'-0" x 15'-0"
vault. clg.

down

loft

am
kitchen

deck

reading
13'-0" x 15'-0"
vault. clg.

open to
below

Quote One®

Cost to build? See page 186
to order complete cost estimate
to build this house in your area!

DESIGN HPT290128

©THE SATER DESIGN
COLLECTION

DESIGN FEATURES

BEDROOMS: 3

BATHROOMS: 2½

FIRST FLOOR: 1,642 Sq. Ft.

SECOND FLOOR: 927 Sq. Ft.

TOTAL: 2,569 Sq. Ft.

WIDTH: 60'-0" DEPTH: 44'-6"

L

LUXURY ABOUNDS in this Floridian home. A recreation room greets you on the first floor. Up the stairs, an open grand room, a bayed nook and a deck stretch across the back of the plan. Two bedrooms occupy the right side of this level and share a full hall bath that includes a double-sink vanity and a separate tub and shower. The master retreat on the upper level pleases with its own reading room, morning kitchen, large walk-in closet and a pampering bath with a double-bowl vanity, whirlpool tub and a shower that opens outside. A private deck allows outdoor enjoyments.

DESIGN HPT290129
©HOME PLANNERS

DESIGN FEATURES

BEDROOMS: 6

BATHROOMS: 5

FIRST FLOOR: 3,166 Sq. Ft.

SECOND FLOOR: 950 Sq. Ft.

TOTAL: 4,116 Sq. Ft.

GUEST HOUSE: 680 Sq. Ft.

WIDTH: 154'-0" DEPTH: 94'-8"

L

A LONG, LOW-PITCHED ROOF distinguishes this Southwestern-style farmhouse design. The tiled entrance leads to a grand dining room and opens to a formal parlor secluded by half-walls. A country kitchen with a cooktop island overlooks the two-story gathering room with its full wall of glass, fireplace and built-in media shelves. The master suite satisfies the most discerning tastes with a raised hearth, an adjacent study or exercise room, access to the wraparound porch, and a bath with a corner whirlpool tub. Rooms upstairs can serve as secondary bedrooms for family members, or can be converted to home office space or used as guest bedrooms.

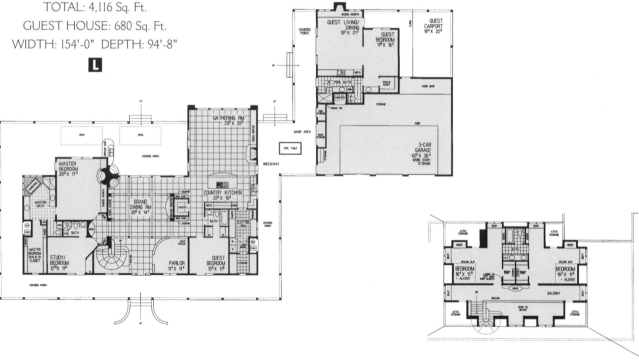

A PLEASANT BLEND OF PAST AND PRESENT,

traditional-style homes offer a melding of elements that draws on both

luxury and comfort. At once formal and friendly, these uniquely

American homes help define the durability of classic architecture. With

bold horizontal lines, massive chimneys, Palladian windows and arched

entries complemented by eclectic blends of stately brick and siding, these

gracious homes eloquently express where we've come from and where we

are today. Presenting flavors of historic architecture such as the hip roof,

keystone arches and a combination of facade materials, the homes in this

section pay homage to the many traditional influences in style and detail-

ing, yet are all utterly progressive.

SHOWN ABOVE:

DESIGN HPT290135

BY FILLMORE

DESIGN GROUP.

SEE PAGE 147 FOR

MORE INFORMATION

ON THIS IMPRESSIVE

TRADITIONAL HOME.

DESIGN HPT290130
©FILLMORE DESIGN GROUP

DESIGN FEATURES
BEDROOMS: 4
BATHROOMS: 3½
TOTAL: 3,818 Sq. Ft.
WIDTH: 107'-4" DEPTH: 68'-7"

THIS SPRAWLING TRADITIONAL FACADE incorporates brick quoins and a cast-stone arched entry to create a design of undeniable style and stature. The living room, with an eight-foot-wide fireplace, full-wall windows and a fourteen-foot ceiling, connects to the family room, which features yet another fireplace and an open wet bar. A study with a fourteen-foot ceiling and a bay window faces the front. The large kitchen is placed between the breakfast area and the formal dining room. A grand master suite includes His and Hers baths, each with a walk-in closet. Right next door, Bedroom 2 is perfect for a nursery. Bedrooms 3 and 4 on the right of the home are separated from the master suite and share a full bath.

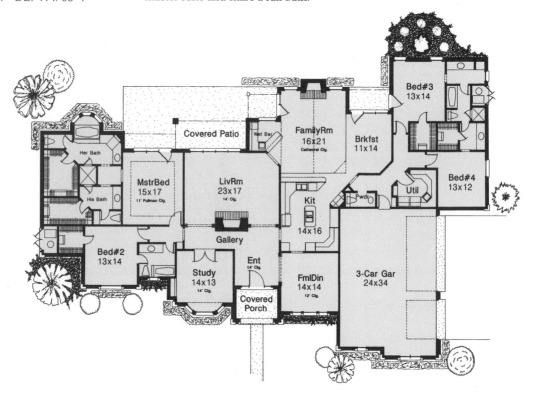

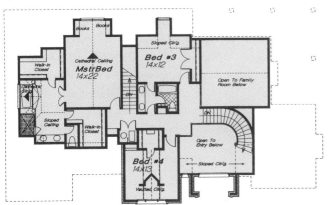

DESIGN FEATURES

BEDROOMS: 4

BATHROOMS: 3½

FIRST FLOOR: 2,506 Sq. Ft.

SECOND FLOOR: 1,415 Sq. Ft.

TOTAL: 6,421 Sq. Ft.

WIDTH: 80'-5"   DEPTH: 50'-4"

DESIGN HPT290131
©FILLMORE DESIGN GROUP

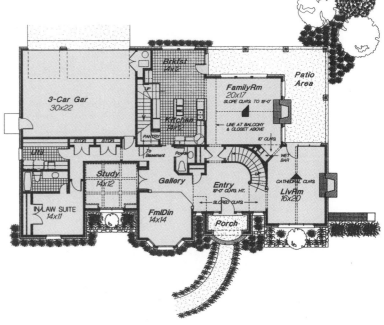

A STATELY TWO-STORY HOME with a gracious, manorly exterior features a large, arched entryway as its focal point. Excellent brick detailing and brick quoins help make this exterior one of a kind. The large, two-story family area is adjacent to the living room with its cathedral ceiling and formal fireplace—a convenient arrangement for entertaining large groups, or just a cozy evening at home. A wrapping patio area allows for dining outdoors. The large kitchen is centrally located, with a second stairway leading to the second floor. The master suite features a volume ceiling and a sitting area overlooking the rear yard. The huge master bath includes two walk-in closets. The upper balcony overlooks the family area and the entryway.

DESIGN HPT290132

©DESIGN BASICS, INC.

A SPECTACULAR VOLUME ENTRY with a curving staircase opens through columns to the formal areas of this home. The sunken living room contains a fireplace, a wet bar and a bowed window overlooking the back property, while the front-facing dining room offers a built-in hutch and a handy servery. The family room, with bookcases surrounding a fireplace, is open to a bayed breakfast nook, and both are easily served from the nearby kitchen. Placed away from the living area of the home, the den provides a quiet retreat and a stunning window. The master suite on the first floor contains a most elegant bath and a huge walk-in closet. Second-floor bedrooms also include walk-in closets and private baths.

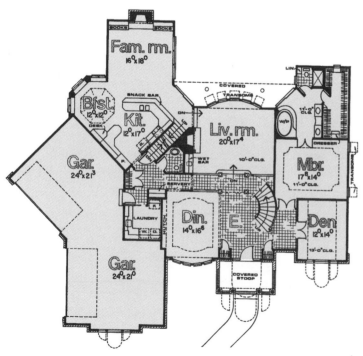

DESIGN FEATURES

BEDROOMS: 4
BATHROOMS: 4½
FIRST FLOOR: 2,617 Sq. Ft.
SECOND FLOOR: 1,072 Sq. Ft.
TOTAL: 3,689 Sq. Ft.
WIDTH: 83'-5" DEPTH: 73'-4"

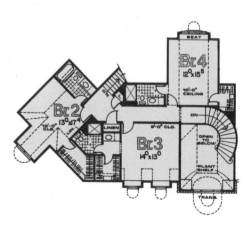

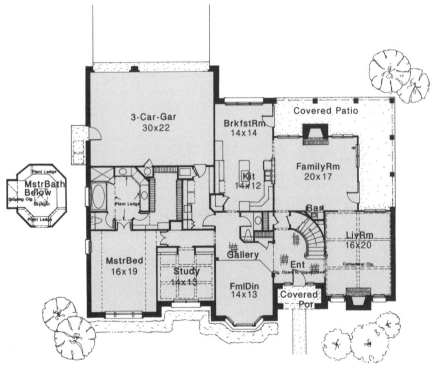

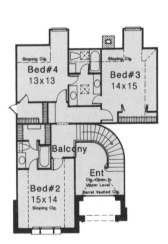

DESIGN HPT290133
©FILLMORE DESIGN GROUP

THIS EXTERIOR IS HIGHLIGHTED with exquisite brick detail and a graceful curving brick arch over the front entrance. Inside, the two-story barrel ceiling and the lovely sweeping stairway highlight the entrance. For entertaining, the living area and family room flow together nicely. Outside, a covered patio provides outdoor enjoyment. A wood-paneled study with beamed ceiling and floor-to-ceiling bookcases sits off the gallery near the secluded master suite. The master bedroom has a vaulted ceiling to allow for the large Palladian window in front. The private bath also contains a tall ceiling with plant ledges surrounding it and a skylight in the center. Three large bedrooms and two baths occupy the second floor.

DESIGN FEATURES
BEDROOMS: 4
BATHROOMS: 3½
FIRST FLOOR: 2,635 Sq. Ft.
SECOND FLOOR: 1,005 Sq. Ft.
TOTAL: 6,240 Sq. Ft.
WIDTH: 73'-0" DEPTH: 59'-10"

DESIGN HPT290134

©DESIGN BASICS, INC.

DESIGN FEATURES

BEDROOMS: 4

BATHROOMS: 4½ + ½

FIRST FLOOR: 2,839 Sq. Ft.

SECOND FLOOR: 1,111 Sq. Ft.

TOTAL: 3,950 Sq. Ft.

WIDTH: 95'-9" DEPTH: 70'-2"

A TWO-STORY FOYER INTRODUCES the formal living zones of this plan—a den with a ten-foot ceiling, a dining room with an adjoining butler's pantry, and a living room with a fireplace and a twelve-foot ceiling. For more casual living, the gathering room shares space with the octagonal breakfast area and the amenity-filled kitchen. Sleeping arrangements include a first-floor master suite, which offers a sitting area with a fireplace, a bath with a corner whirlpool tub and compartmented toilet, and an extensive closet. The second floor holds three bedrooms, each with a walk-in closet and private bath.

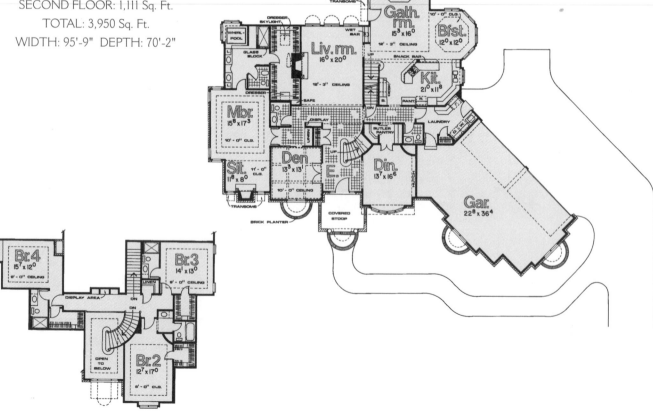

DESIGN HPT290135

©FILLMORE DESIGN GROUP

DESIGN FEATURES

BEDROOMS: 4

BATHROOMS: 3½

FIRST FLOOR: 2,728 Sq. Ft.

SECOND FLOOR: 1,008 Sq. Ft.

TOTAL: 3,736 Sq. Ft.

WIDTH: 70'-0" DEPTH: 56'-7"

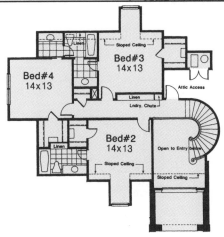

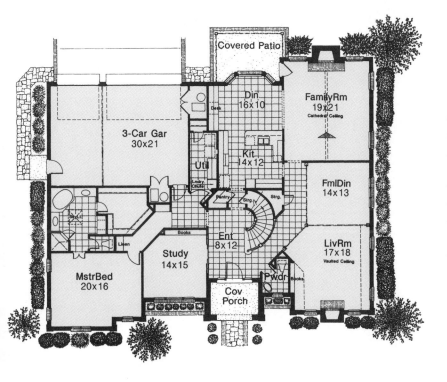

CAST-STONE ARCHES, dentiled eaves and brick quoins harmonize on the facade of this traditional European design. A breathtaking, two-story entry reveals a curving stairway and balcony. The adjoining open spaces of the formal dining room and living room with a brick fireplace offer warm hospitality to guests. The family room provides another fireplace, a cathedral ceiling and access to the covered patio. To the front of the home, a study offers built-in bookshelves. The master suite features a pampering bath with dual vanities, a large tub and a private water closet. Three family bedrooms, each with a walk-in closet and access to a full bath, are located upstairs. A three-car garage is located at the rear of the home.

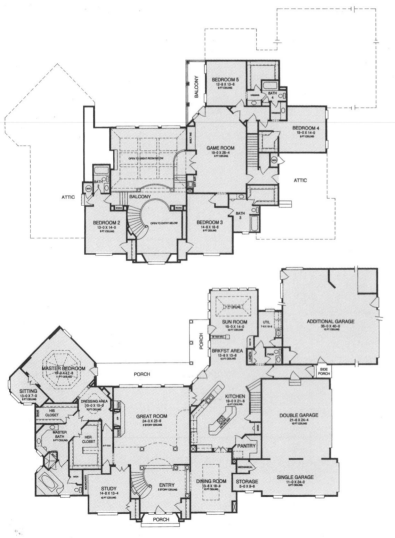

DESIGN HPT290136
©LARRY E. BELK DESIGNS

A RICHLY DETAILED entrance sets the elegant tone of this luxurious design. Rising gracefully from the two-story foyer, the staircase is a fine prelude to the great room beyond, where a fantastic span of windows on the back wall overlooks the rear grounds. The dining room is located off the entry and has a lovely coffered ceiling. The kitchen, breakfast room and sun room are conveniently grouped for casual entertaining. The elaborate master suite enjoys a coffered ceiling, private sitting room and spa-style bath. The second level consists of four bedrooms with private baths and a large game room featuring a rear stair.

DESIGN FEATURES
BEDROOMS: 5
BATHROOMS: 4½
FIRST FLOOR: 3,722 Sq. Ft.
SECOND FLOOR: 1,859 Sq. Ft.
TOTAL: 5,581 Sq. Ft.
WIDTH: 127'-10" DEPTH: 83'-9"

L

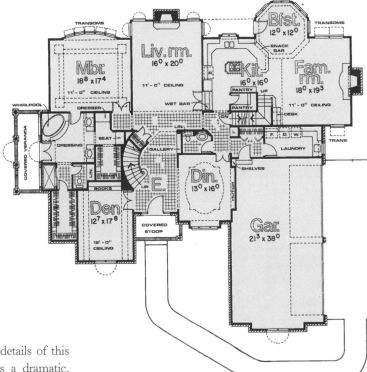

DESIGN HPT290137

©DESIGN BASICS, INC.

THE SOPHISTICATED LINES and brick details of this house are stunning enhancements. The entry surveys a dramatic, curved staircase. French doors open to the den, where a tiered ceiling and a bookcase wall provide a lofty ambiance. Large gatherings are easily accommodated in the dining room. The living room enjoys an eleven-foot ceiling and a fireplace flanked by transom windows. For more casual living, the family room includes a raised-hearth fireplace and a built-in desk. The gourmet kitchen provides two pantries, an island cooktop, a wrapping counter, a snack bar and private stairs to the second level. Four bedrooms include a pampering master suite on the first floor and three family bedrooms upstairs.

DESIGN FEATURES

BEDROOMS: 4

BATHROOMS: 3½

FIRST FLOOR: 2,789 Sq. Ft.

SECOND FLOOR: 1,038 Sq. Ft.

TOTAL: 3,827 Sq. Ft.

WIDTH: 78'-0" DEPTH: 73'-8"

DESIGN HPT290138

©ALAN MASCORD DESIGN
ASSOCIATES, INC.

SPECTACULAR IS THE WORD for this "Texas" traditional home! Note the two-story foyer with its split stairway and columns framing the openings to the living and dining rooms. The dramatic master suite is conveniently found on the main floor. The fireplace serves both the bedroom and the spa area. Three additional bedrooms are provided upstairs, two with their own bathrooms. The rear bedroom would make an ideal library.

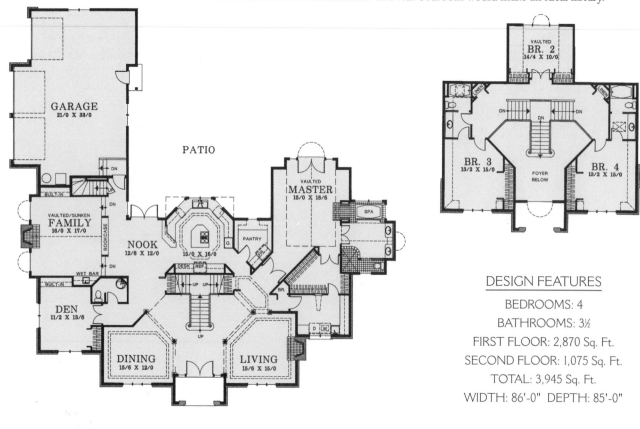

DESIGN FEATURES

BEDROOMS: 4

BATHROOMS: 3½

FIRST FLOOR: 2,870 Sq. Ft.

SECOND FLOOR: 1,075 Sq. Ft.

TOTAL: 3,945 Sq. Ft.

WIDTH: 86'-0" DEPTH: 85'-0"

DESIGN HPT290139
©FILLMORE DESIGN GROUP

THE DISTINCTIVE COVERED ENTRY to this stunning manor leads to a gracious porch with impressive two-story semi-circular fanlights. The foyer leads to the study, formal dining room, formal living room and master suite. The numerous amenities in the kitchen include an island workstation and built-in pantry. The breakfast room features a cone ceiling. The luxurious master suite, secluded in its own wing, is complete with a covered patio. The master bedroom has a huge walk-in closet. Upstairs are three bedrooms, two baths and a future playroom area.

DESIGN FEATURES

BEDROOMS: 4
BATHROOMS: 3½
FIRST FLOOR: 2,997 Sq. Ft.
SECOND FLOOR: 983 Sq. Ft.
TOTAL: 3,980 Sq. Ft.
WIDTH: 89'-4" DEPTH: 71'-0"

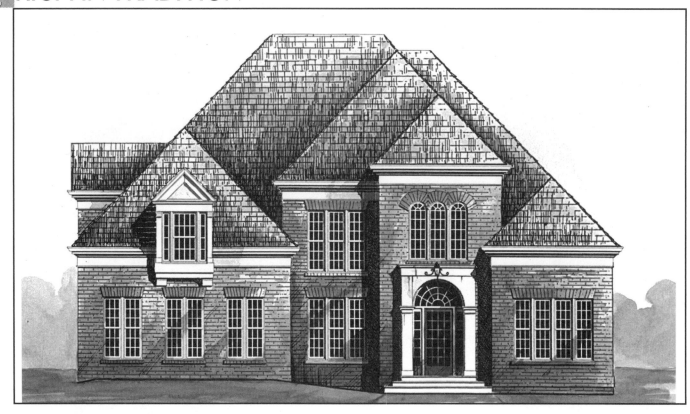

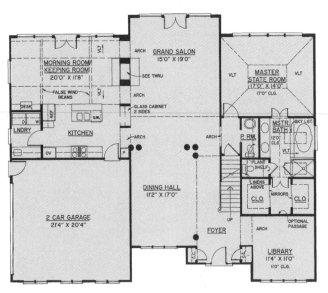

DESIGN HPT290140

©ARCHIVAL DESIGNS, INC.

NESTED, HIPPED GABLES CREATE a dramatic effect in this beautiful two-story brick home. The arched doorway is echoed in the triple clerestory window that lights the two-story foyer. Columns decorate the formal dining room, which is open to the two-story grand room with a fireplace. The master suite is located downstairs for privacy, while upstairs, three secondary bedrooms are joined by a gallery overlooking the grand room.

DESIGN FEATURES

BEDROOMS: 4

BATHROOMS: 3½

FIRST FLOOR: 1,809 Sq. Ft.

SECOND FLOOR: 898 Sq. Ft.

TOTAL: 2,707 Sq. Ft.

WIDTH: 54'-4" DEPTH: 46'-0"

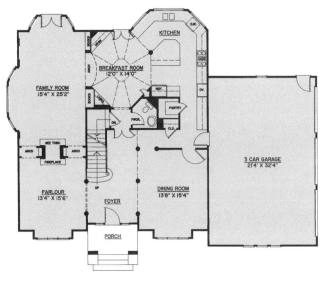

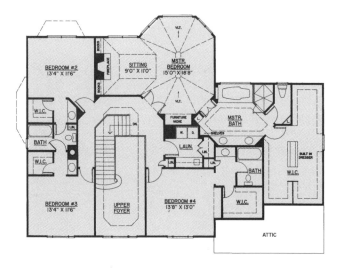

DESIGN HPT290141

©ARCHIVAL DESIGNS, INC.

Wʜᴀᴛ ʙᴇᴛᴛᴇʀ ᴡᴀʏ ᴛᴏ ꜱᴛᴀʀᴛ—or even to end—your day than in the beautiful octangonal breakfast room within this masterful design? It opens to a curved island kitchen, with plenty of room for even the messiest of cooks, and to the cozy family room. This room provides access, via French doors, to the outside and shares a fireplace with the front parlor. A formal dining room and a powder room complete the first floor. On the second floor, the master bedroom offers the same romantic design, as well as a fireplace in the large sitting area. It also includes a luxurious private bath with twin walk-in closets. Two family bedrooms with walk-in closets share a full bath while another bedroom features its own private bath.

DESIGN FEATURES

BEDROOMS: 4
BATHROOMS: 3½
FIRST FLOOR: 1,597 Sq. Ft.
SECOND FLOOR: 1,859 Sq. Ft.
TOTAL: 3,456 Sq. Ft.
WIDTH: 62'-0" DEPTH: 46'-0"

DESIGN HPT290142

©FRANK BETZ
ASSOCIATES, INC.

DESIGN FEATURES

BEDROOMS: 4

BATHROOMS: 3

FIRST FLOOR: 1,761 Sq. Ft.

SECOND FLOOR: 580 Sq. Ft.

TOTAL: 2,341 Sq. Ft.

BONUS ROOM: 276 Sq. Ft.

WIDTH: 56'-0" DEPTH: 47'-6"

Quote One®

Cost to build? See page 186
to order complete cost estimate
to build this house in your area!

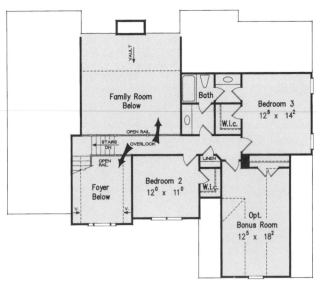

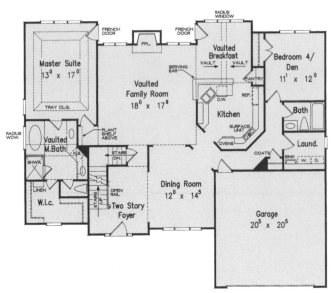

DECORATIVE ARCHES AND QUOINS give this home a wonderful curb appeal that matches its comfortable interior. The two-story foyer is bathed in natural light as it leads to the formal dining room and beyond to the counter-filled kitchen and the vaulted breakfast nook. A den, or possible fourth bedroom, is tucked away at the rear for privacy and includes a full bath. Located downstairs, also for privacy, is a spacious master suite with a luxurious private bath. Two family bedrooms and a full bath are located on the second floor, as well as a balcony that looks down to the family room and the foyer. An optional bonus room is available for expanding at a later date. Please specify basement or crawlspace foundation when ordering.

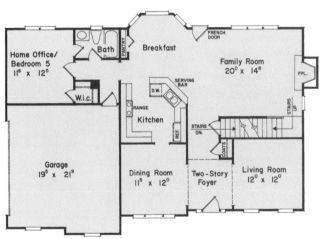

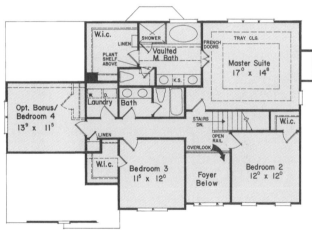

DESIGN HPT290143

©FRANK BETZ
ASSOCIATES, INC.

QUOTE ONE®

Cost to build? See page 186
to order complete cost estimate
to build this house in your area!

A GRACEFUL FRONT PORCH with a French-door entry welcomes guests to this traditional three-bedroom home. Living quarters downstairs include a well-designed eat-in kitchen with a great deal of counter space, a formal dining area, spacious family room, laundry room and powder room. All three bedrooms reside upstairs. The master bedroom features a vast walk-in closet and a grand private bath with two vanities, a shower stall and a separate bathtub. The additional bedrooms each have considerable closets and share a bathroom. Please specify basement or crawlspace foundation when ordering.

DESIGN FEATURES

BEDROOMS: 4

BATHROOMS: 3

FIRST FLOOR: 1,294 Sq. Ft.

SECOND FLOOR: 1,067 Sq. Ft.

TOTAL: 2,361 Sq. Ft.

BONUS ROOM: 168 Sq. Ft.

WIDTH: 54'-4" DEPTH: 37'-6"

DESIGN FEATURES

BEDROOMS: 3

BATHROOMS: 3½

FIRST FLOOR: 2,429 Sq. Ft.

SECOND FLOOR: 654 Sq. Ft.

TOTAL: 3,083 Sq. Ft.

BONUS ROOM: 420 Sq. Ft.

WIDTH: 63'-6" DEPTH: 71'-4"

KEYSTONES THAT CAP EACH WINDOW, a terrace that dresses up the entrance, and a bay-windowed turret add up to a totally refined exterior of this home. Inside, open planning employs columns to define the foyer, dining room and two-story family room. The first-floor master suite is designed with every amenity to answer your needs. Rounding out the first floor are the kitchen, breakfast nook and keeping room. The second floor contains two bedrooms, each with a private bath and walk-in closet, and an optional bonus room. Please specify basement or crawlspace foundation when ordering.

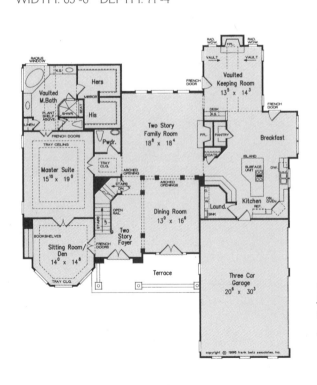

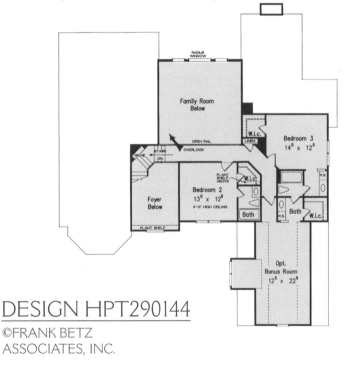

DESIGN HPT290144

©FRANK BETZ
ASSOCIATES, INC.

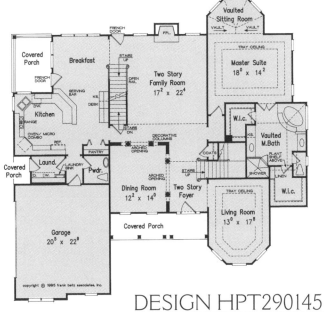

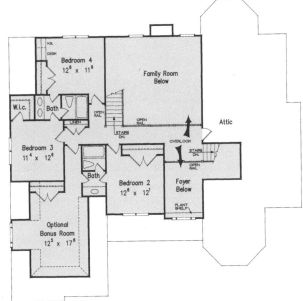

DESIGN HPT290145

©FRANK BETZ
ASSOCIATES, INC.

IT WILL BE A PLEASURE TO COME HOME to this traditional French design after a long day at work. From the pleasing covered porch, the two-story foyer leads through an arched opening to the formal dining room and also to the charming bayed living room. A convenient stairway leads up to the second floor. The master suite is tucked away on the first floor, with its own vaulted sitting room, walk-in closet and spacious bath. The two-story family room with a fireplace and rear views rounds out the main level. Three more bedrooms and two baths, plus an optional bonus room (which would be perfect for a home theater), complete the upper level. Please specify basement or crawlspace foundation when ordering.

DESIGN FEATURES

BEDROOMS: 4
BATHROOMS: 3½
FIRST FLOOR: 2,294 Sq. Ft.
SECOND FLOOR: 869 Sq. Ft.
TOTAL: 3,163 Sq. Ft.
BONUS ROOM: 309 Sq. Ft.
WIDTH: 63'-6" DEPTH: 63'-0"

DESIGN HPT290146

©STEPHEN FULLER, INC.

THIS ATTRACTIVE HOME has a rather unique floor plan that works well—especially for those who like to entertain in style. Enter through double doors and find a bedroom or study immediately to the right. Walk straight ahead through columns to find is a large, open area, defined by more columns, that holds the formal dining room and the great room (a fireplace and built-in bookshelves are amenities here). The sleeping quarters are all arranged along the right wing of the plan. This home is designed with a walkout basement foundation.

DESIGN FEATURES

BEDROOMS: 3

BATHROOMS: 3½

TOTAL: 2,973 Sq. Ft.

WIDTH: 75'-0" DEPTH: 70'-0"

© 1998 Donald A. Gardner, Inc.

DECK

KIT.
11-10 x 14-0

BRKFST.
10-0 x 14-0

LIVING RM.
16-4 x 20-0

(cathedral ceiling)

fireplace

MASTER
BED RM.
17-0 x 14-0

linen

master
bath

lin.

walk-in
closet

bath

cl

DINING
13-0 x 14-4

FOYER
6-8 x
13-2

down

railing

BED RM.
12-0 x 13-0

UTIL.
7-4 x
9-0

cl

cl

d

w

bath

storage

BED RM./
STUDY
13-0 x 13-0

PORCH

© 1998 Donald A Gardner, Inc.

GARAGE
22-0 x 22-8

storage

DESIGN FEATURES

BEDROOMS: 5

BATHROOMS: 5½

MAIN LEVEL: 2,297 Sq. Ft.

LOWER LEVEL: 1,212 Sq. Ft.

TOTAL: 3,509 Sq. Ft.

WIDTH: 70'-10" DEPTH: 69'-0"

DESIGN HPT290147

DONALD A. GARDNER
ARCHITECTS, INC.

A VARIETY OF EXTERIOR MATERIALS and interesting windows combine with an unusual floor plan to make this an exceptional home. It is designed for a sloping lot, with full living quarters on the main level, but with two extra bedrooms and a family room added to the lower level. A covered porch showcases a wonderful dining-room window and an attractive front door. The living room, enhanced by a fireplace, adjoins the dining room for easy entertaining. The island kitchen and a bayed breakfast room are to the left. Three bedrooms on this level include one that could serve as a study and a master suite with dual vanities, a garden tub and a walk-in closet. A deck on this floor covers the patio off the lower-level family room, which has its own fireplace.

COVERED
PATIO

BED RM.
13-8 x 14-0

bath

cl

cl

cl

pd.
rm.

FAMILY RM.
16-4 x 20-0

fireplace

cl

lin.

BED RM.
14-8 x 12-4

bath

storage

up

© 1998 Donald A Gardner, Inc.

STORAGE
(unfinished)

FINELY CRAFTED PORCHES—front, side and rear—make this home a classic in traditional Southern living. Past the large French doors, the impressive foyer is flanked by the formal living and dining rooms. Beyond the stair is a vaulted great room with an expanse of windows, a fireplace and built-in bookcases. From here, the breakfast room and kitchen are easily accessible and open to a side porch. The master suite provides a large bath, two spacious closets, a fireplace and a private entry that opens to the covered rear porch. The second floor contains three bedrooms with private bath access and a playroom. This home is designed with a walkout basement foundation.

DESIGN HPT290148

©STEPHEN FULLER, INC.

DESIGN FEATURES

BEDROOMS: 4

BATHROOMS: 3½

FIRST FLOOR: 2,380 Sq. Ft.

SECOND FLOOR: 1,295 Sq. Ft.

TOTAL: 3,675 Sq. Ft.

WIDTH: 77'-4" DEPTH: 58'-4"

QUOTE ONE®

Cost to build? See page 186 to order complete cost estimate to build this house in your area!

DESIGN HPT290149

©LARRY JAMES &
ASSOCIATES, INC.

COUNTRY ELEMENTS GRACEFULLY

mingle in this four-bedroom home, with dormers and four columns supporting the front porch. Three transom-covered entries greet visitors at the porch—the main entry and two French doors leading to the dining room and a secondary bedroom/study, respectively. The elegance continues inside with columns defining the dining area from the entry. The nearby kitchen features a useful work island. The breakfast nook fills with light from the box-bay window and includes access to the backyard. Two additional French doors access the backyard from the great room and are beautifully set around the warming fireplace. The master suite enjoys a ribbon of windows viewing the backyard and a sumptuous bath with a separate shower, garden tub and walk-in closet. Two family bedrooms share a full bath with the playroom on the second level. Expansion on the second floor is possible in the future. Please specify basement, crawlspace or slab foundation when ordering.

DESIGN FEATURES

BEDROOMS: 4

BATHROOMS: 2½

FIRST FLOOR: 1,906 Sq. Ft.

SECOND FLOOR: 763 Sq. Ft.

TOTAL: 2,669 Sq. Ft.

BONUS SPACE: 655 Sq. Ft.

WIDTH: 73'-0" DEPTH: 44'-0"

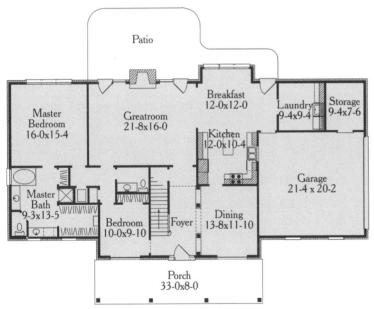

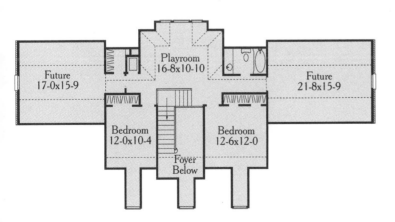

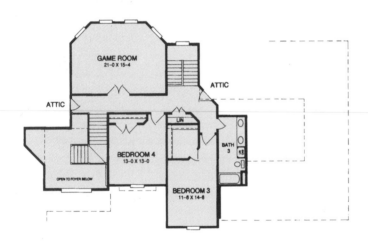

DESIGN HPT290150
©LARRY E. BELK DESIGNS

PUT A LITTLE LUXURY into your life with this fine brick home. A great room with a fireplace and expansive windows provides the perfect spot for gatherings of all sorts. A large study nearby creates a quiet environment for working at home. The kitchen has a large cooktop island and a convenient walk-in pantry. In the dining room, bumped-out windows shed light on entertaining. The first-floor master suite has its own fireplace and a pampering bath. A second bedroom with a private bath is nearby. Upstairs, two more bedrooms, a full bath and an expansive game room complete the plan.

DESIGN FEATURES

BEDROOMS: 4
BATHROOMS: 3½
FIRST FLOOR: 2,648 Sq. Ft.
SECOND FLOOR: 1,102 Sq. Ft.
TOTAL: 3,750 Sq. Ft.
WIDTH: 91'-6" DEPTH: 46'-10"

L

A STYLE THAT CONSCIOUSLY STRIVES FOR MODERNITY

and artistic expression, contemporary architecture borrows heavily from Modernist and International styles. The emphasis on the future rather than the past is one of this style's principal characteristics. Details such as concrete, smooth-faced stone, large glass openings and geometric shapes define the style and give it special flavor. Other typical features include terraces, patios and private balconies. Contemporary design caters to the pace of today's more frenetic lifestyle. With open spaces, efficient kitchens, many large bathrooms and multi-purpose rooms to provide the space for a variety of activities, this style adds adaptability to its impressive description. Distinctive, bold and elegantly eclectic, the plans in this section are in a class by themselves.

SHOWN ABOVE:

DESIGN HPT290165

BY LIVING CONCEPTS

HOME PLANNING.

SEE PAGE 178 FOR

MORE INFORMATION

ON THIS MODERN-DAY

MARVEL OF A HOME.

DESIGN HPT290151

©BRELAND & FARMER
DESIGNERS, INC.

DESIGN FEATURES

BEDROOMS: 4

BATHROOMS: 2

TOTAL: 2,396 Sq. Ft.

WIDTH: 72'-0" DEPTH: 60'-0"

LONG AND LOW, but sporting a high roofline, this one-story plan offers the best in family livability. The recessed entry opens to an entry hall that leads to a huge living area with a fireplace. An angled eating area is close by and connects to the galley-style kitchen. The formal dining area also connects to the kitchen, but retains access to the entry hall for convenience. Family bedrooms are on the left side of the plan and share a full bath. The master suite sits behind the two-car garage and is graced by patio access and a fine bath. Note the large storage area in the garage. Please specify basement, crawlspace or slab foundation when ordering.

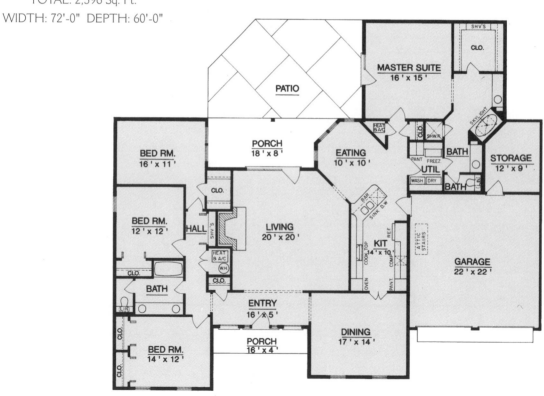

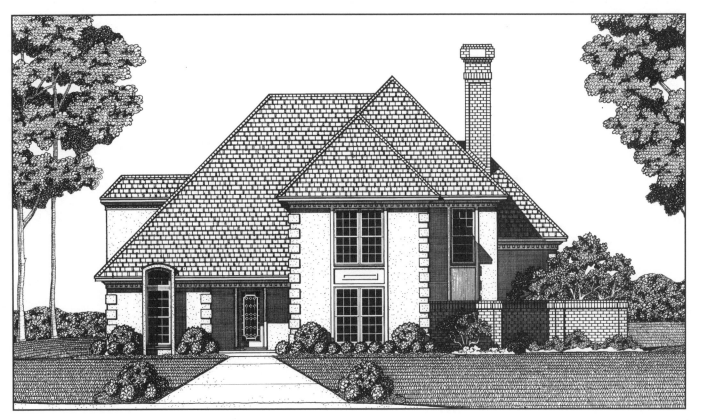

DESIGN FEATURES

BEDROOMS: 4
BATHROOMS: 2½
FIRST FLOOR: 1,708 Sq. Ft.
SECOND FLOOR: 811 Sq. Ft.
TOTAL: 2,519 Sq. Ft.
WIDTH: 52'-0" DEPTH: 72'-0"

CORNER QUOINS, tall windows and multiple rooflines add a unique appeal to this design. Inside, the formal dining room features a tray ceiling and double doors that open to the kitchen. An eating nook shares a snack bar with the kitchen and overlooks the rear patio. The living room embraces a fireplace, built-in bookshelves and cabinets. Sleeping quarters consist of a master suite on the first level and three bedrooms on the second level. Walk-in closets are provided in the master suite and two of the family bedrooms. Please specify basement, crawlspace or slab foundation when ordering.

DESIGN HPT290152

©BRELAND & FARMER
DESIGNERS, INC.

Photo by Michael Lowry Photography

DESIGN HPT290153
©ERIC S. BROWN'S PALLADIAN
DESIGN COLLECTION

WITH SLEEK LINES AND GENTLE ARCHES, this Mediterranean beauty brings a new brand of dignity and a dash of the past to Sun Country style. The entry leads to an open foyer and formal parlor. Double doors open from a gallery hall to the secluded study, which could serve as a home office. To the other side of the parlor, an elegant arrangement of columns and arches define the formal dining room. The gourmet kitchen serves an eating bar and morning nook. One of the suites is a detached guest house with a bay living room overlooking the rear yard. On the opposite side of the plan, a rambling master suite features two walk-in closets, a dressing area, separate vanities, an oversized shower and a privacy garden.

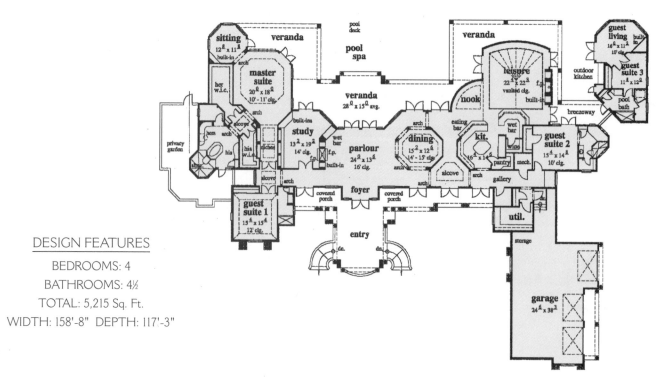

DESIGN FEATURES

BEDROOMS: 4
BATHROOMS: 4½
TOTAL: 5,215 Sq. Ft.
WIDTH: 158'-8"   DEPTH: 117'-3"

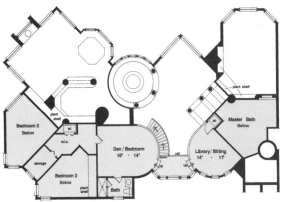

DESIGN HPT290154
©HOME DESIGN
SERVICES, INC.

DESIGN FEATURES

BEDROOMS: 4

BATHROOMS: 4½

FIRST FLOOR: 3,236 Sq. Ft.

SECOND FLOOR: 494 Sq. Ft.

TOTAL: 3,730 Sq. Ft.

WIDTH: 80'-0" DEPTH: 89'-10"

I<small>F</small> <small>YOU</small> <small>WANT</small> <small>TO</small> B<small>UILD</small> a home light years ahead of most other designs, non-traditional, yet addresses every need for your family, this showcase home is for you. From the moment you walk into this home, you are confronted with wonderful interior architecture that reflects modern, yet refined taste. The exterior says contemporary; the interior creates special excitement. Note the special rounded corners found throughout the home and the many amenities. The master suite is especially appealing with a fireplace and grand bath. Upstairs are a library/sitting room and a very private den or guest bedroom.

Photo by Oscar Thompson Photography

This home, as shown in the photograph, may differ from the actual blueprints. For more detailed information, please check the floor plans carefully.

DESIGN HPT290155

©ERIC S. BROWN'S PALLADIAN
DESIGN COLLECTION

THIS AWARD-WINNING design is arranged in a flowing, open layout that uses richly detailed architectural elements to define the living and dining spaces. Comfortable living is guaranteed in the open leisure room, surrounded by walls of glass. An open skylight tops a secluded niche of the veranda, guarded by a privacy wall, creating an ideal place to enjoy meals outside. The leisure room opens to a morning nook and eating bar, both served by the kitchen. The spacious guest suite boasts a walk-in closet, full bath with a garden tub, and sliding glass door access to the veranda. The lavish master suite offers a private bath that features separate vanities.

DESIGN FEATURES

BEDROOMS: 3

BATHROOMS: 3½

TOTAL: 4,575 Sq. Ft.

WIDTH: 100'-0" DEPTH: 126'-0"

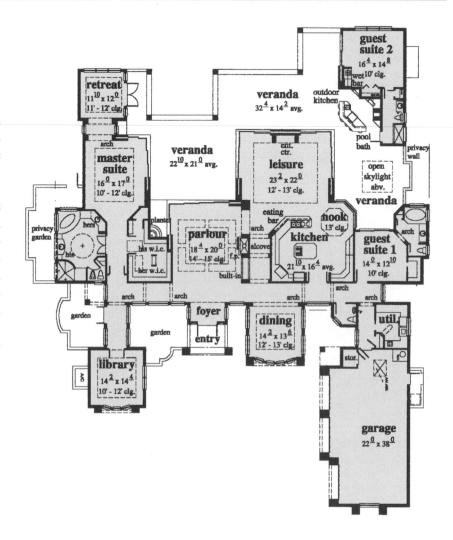

Photo by Oscar Thompson Photography

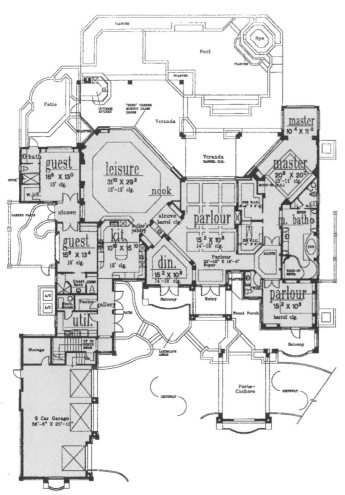

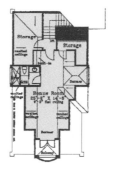

DESIGN HPT290156
©ERIC S. BROWN'S PALLADIAN
DESIGN COLLECTION

STUCCO AND SHINGLES ADORN the beautiful facade of this award-winning plan. A covered port cochere shelters guests from the elements and provides a proper introduction to a home that it will be easy to fall in love with. A fifteen-foot ceiling in the formal parlor creates a sense of grandeur, enhanced by open views. A butler's pantry connects the kitchen with the formal dining room. The master suite offers a private parlor that easily converts to a study. The private bath includes a walk-in shower, separate vanities and a glorious whirlpool tub with a garden view.

DESIGN FEATURES
BEDROOMS: 4
BATHROOMS: 4½
FIRST FLOOR: 4,762 Sq. Ft.
SECOND FLOOR: 775 Sq. Ft.
TOTAL: 5,537 Sq. Ft.
WIDTH: 100'-0" DEPTH: 130'-0"

DESIGN HPT290157
©HOME DESIGN SERVICES, INC.

A GRACEFUL DESIGN sets this charming home apart from the ordinary and transcends the commonplace. From the foyer, the dining room branches off the sunny living room, setting a lovely backdrop for entertaining. Casual living is the focus in the oversized family room, where sliding doors open to the patio and the eat-in, gourmet kitchen is open for easy conversation. Two family bedrooms and a cabana bath are just off the family room. The master suite has a cozy fireplace in the sitting area, and twin closets and a compartmented bath. A large covered patio adds to the living area.

DESIGN FEATURES

BEDROOMS: 3
BATHROOMS: 2½
TOTAL: 2,656 Sq. Ft.
WIDTH: 92'-0" DEPTH: 69'-0"

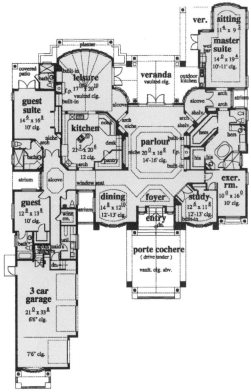

DESIGN FEATURES

BEDROOMS: 4

BATHROOMS: 5½

APARTMENT: 525 Sq. Ft.

TOTAL: 4,585 Sq. Ft.

WIDTH: 84'-0" DEPTH: 129'-8"

DESIGN HPT290158
©ERIC S. BROWN'S PALLADIAN
DESIGN COLLECTION

STRAIGHTFORWARD LINES, a wraparound veranda, high-pitched rooflines and a host of atriums blur the separation between the living areas of this stunning stucco home and the natural world that surrounds it. The dining room faces the front garden. A beautiful bowed window and tray ceiling help to define this formal room. The leisure room provides access to the rear veranda. The kitchen boasts an eat-in table in the morning nook. The master suite is a truly opulent retreat—the bedroom provides a wet bar, sitting area, tray ceiling, bay window and doors to the veranda and outdoor kitchen.

CONTEMPORARY SPLENDOR

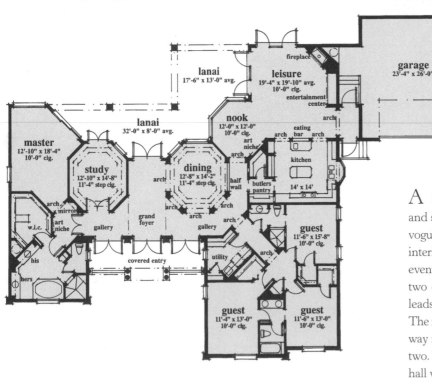

A CAREFUL BLEND of horizontal siding and stucco accents lends a continental appeal to this voguish home. Cutting-edge style continues with an interior plan designed to accommodate traditional events as well as casual living. A grand foyer opens to two octagonal formal rooms and a gallery hall that leads to the master suite and a guest and living wing. The master suite features a dressing area with a three-way mirror, art niche and walk-in closet designed for two. Three guest suites share two baths and a private hall with a laundry.

DESIGN FEATURES

BEDROOMS: 4

BATHROOMS: 3

TOTAL: 3,215 Sq. Ft.

WIDTH: 104'-4"   DEPTH: 74'-6"

DESIGN HPT290159

©THE SATER DESIGN
COLLECTION

DESIGN HPT290160

©THE SATER DESIGN
COLLECTION

THIS DYNAMIC EXTERIOR
invites you in through its columned entry.
Inside, the living room and dining room open
to a covered rear lanai; built-ins line one wall of
the adjacent study, which also opens to the
lanai. A resplendent master suite occupies the
left wing and provides a private garden, raised
whirlpool tub, two walk-in closets and a sitting
area. A leisure room to the rear of the plan features a fireplace and a built-in entertainment
center. The gourmet kitchen shares an eating
bar with the breakfast nook. Other special
amenities include art display niches, a wet bar
and a computer center.

DESIGN FEATURES

BEDROOMS: 4

BATHROOMS: 4

TOTAL: 3,036 Sq. Ft.

WIDTH: 88'-0" DEPTH: 119'-0"

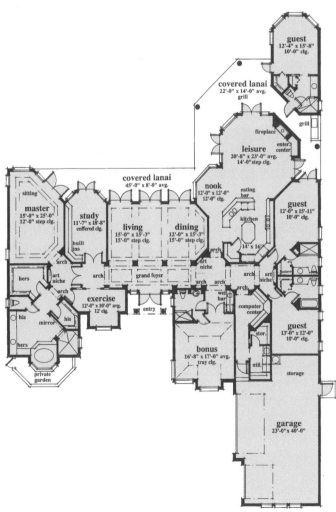

DESIGN FEATURES

BEDROOMS: 3

BATHROOMS: 2½

FIRST FLOOR: 1,954 Sq. Ft.

SECOND FLOOR: 1,308 Sq. Ft.

TOTAL: 3,262 Sq. Ft.

WIDTH: 69'-0" DEPTH: 60'-6"

L

THIS PLAN REAPS PLENTY OF COMPLIMENTS for the sensational entry. Inside, the floor plan enjoys a large, two-story entry which leads on the right to the den with built-ins and a private deck. Straight ahead and down a few steps are the main living areas: the two-story formal living room with a fireplace; the dining room, kitchen and nook, all with tray vaulted ceilings; and the family room with another fireplace and more built-ins. Among three bedrooms on the second floor, the master suite offers a wealth of amenities.

DESIGN HPT290161

©ALAN MASCORD DESIGN ASSOCIATES, INC.

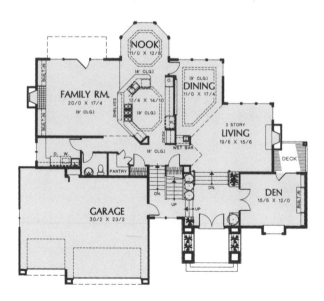

DESIGN HPT290162

©ALAN MASCORD DESIGN
ASSOCIATES, INC.

CLEAN LINES, A HIPPED ROOF and a high, recessed entry define this sleek contemporary home. For informal entertaining, gather in the multi-windowed family room with its step-down wet bar and warming fireplace. The open kitchen will delight everyone with its center cooktop island, corner sink and adjacent breakfast nook. Enter the grand master suite through double doors and take special note of the see-through fireplace between the bedroom and bath. An additional see-through fireplace is located between the living room and den. Two family bedrooms both directly access a compartmented bath.

DESIGN FEATURES

BEDROOMS: 3
BATHROOMS: 2½
FIRST FLOOR: 2,375 Sq. Ft.
SECOND FLOOR: 762 Sq. Ft.
TOTAL: 3,137 Sq. Ft.
WIDTH: 73'-0" DEPTH: 64'-6"

L

CONTEMPORARY SPLENDOR

DRAMATIC ON THE HIGHEST LEVEL,
this spectacular plan offers a recessed entry, double rows of multi-pane windows and two dormers over the garage. On the inside, formal living and dining areas reside to the right of the foyer and are separated from it by columns. A private den is also accessed from the foyer through double doors. The family room with a fireplace to the rear adjoins the breakfast nook and attached island kitchen. The master suite is on the first floor to separate it from family bedrooms. Bonus space over the garage can be developed at a later time.

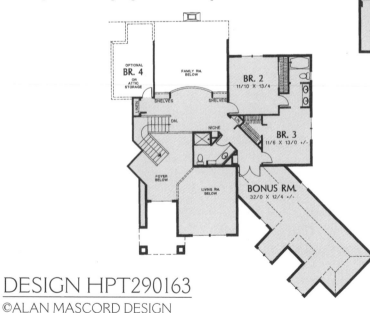

DESIGN HPT290163

©ALAN MASCORD DESIGN
ASSOCIATES, INC.

DESIGN FEATURES

BEDROOMS: 3

BATHROOMS: 3½

FIRST FLOOR: 2,270 Sq. Ft.

SECOND FLOOR: 788 Sq. Ft.

TOTAL: 3,058 Sq. Ft.

WIDTH: 84'-9" DEPTH: 76'-2"

L

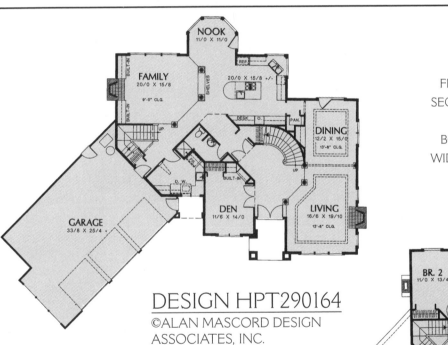

DESIGN FEATURES

BEDROOMS: 3
BATHROOMS: 2½
FIRST FLOOR: 2,148 Sq. Ft.
SECOND FLOOR: 1,300 Sq. Ft.
TOTAL: 3,448 Sq. Ft.
BONUS ROOM: 444 Sq. Ft.
WIDTH: 86'-0" DEPTH: 73'-0"

DESIGN HPT290164
©ALAN MASCORD DESIGN
ASSOCIATES, INC.

LUXURY ABOUNDS in this magnificent contemporary plan. The entry foyer gives way to a den on the left and formal living and dining rooms on the right. A curving staircase leads upstairs to the master suite and two family bedrooms sharing a full bath. The rear of the plan holds a family room separated from the kitchen/nook area by built-in shelves. A back staircase here makes the upstairs even more accessible. Note special features such as the three-car garage, prep island in the kitchen and the bonus room.

HERE'S AN UPSCALE, multi-level plan with expansive rear views. The first floor provides an open living and dining area, defined by decorative columns and enhanced by natural light from tall windows. A breakfast area with a lovely triple window opens to a sun room, which allows light to pour into the gourmet kitchen. The master suite features a tray ceiling in the bedroom, two walk-in closets and an elegant private vestibule leading to a lavish bath. Upstairs, a reading loft overlooks the great room and leads to a sleeping area with two suites.

DESIGN HPT290165
©LIVING CONCEPTS HOME PLANNING

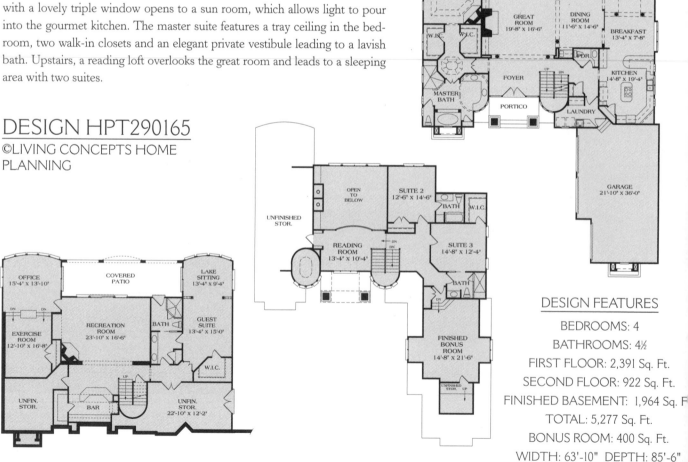

DESIGN FEATURES

BEDROOMS: 4

BATHROOMS: 4½

FIRST FLOOR: 2,391 Sq. Ft.

SECOND FLOOR: 922 Sq. Ft.

FINISHED BASEMENT: 1,964 Sq. F

TOTAL: 5,277 Sq. Ft.

BONUS ROOM: 400 Sq. Ft.

WIDTH: 63'-10" DEPTH: 85'-6"

DESIGN FEATURES

BEDROOMS: 3

BATHROOMS: 2½

FIRST FLOOR: 2,145 Sq. Ft.

SECOND FLOOR: 1,342 Sq. Ft.

TOTAL: 3,487 Sq. Ft.

WIDTH: 79'-6" DEPTH: 71'-2"

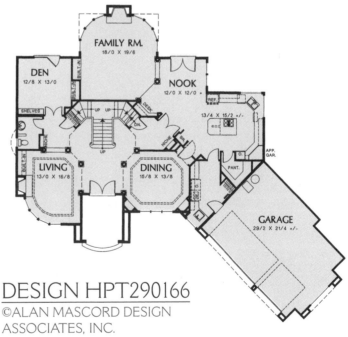

DESIGN HPT290166
©ALAN MASCORD DESIGN
ASSOCIATES, INC.

A DYNAMIC FLOOR PLAN is housed in this elegant exterior. Enter the foyer and find glass-walled living and dining rooms to the left and the right. Straight ahead, the gracious family room sports a fireplace with high windows flanking each side. Columned arches lead into the bumped-out nook with double doors opening to the rear grounds. An L-shaped kitchen features a double-windowed corner sink, a large walk-in pantry and a convenient cooktop/prep island. A den with built-ins and shelves and a sizable laundry room complete the first floor. Upstairs, double doors open to an master suite that offers a cozy fireplace and a pampering bath with a relaxing spa tub and giant walk-in closet. Two family bedrooms and a full bath complete the second floor.

THIS FRESH AND INNOVATIVE design creates unbeatable ambiance. Octagon-shaped rooms, columns and flowing spaces will delight all. The breakfast nook and family room both open to a patio—a perfect arrangement for informal entertaining. The dining room is sure to please with elegant pillars separating it from the sunken living room. A media room delights with its shape and convenience to the nearby kitchen—perfect for snack runs. A private garden surrounds the master bath and its spa tub and enormous walk-in closet. The master bedroom is enchanting with a fireplace and access to the outdoors. Additional family bedrooms come in a variety of different shapes and sizes.

DESIGN HPT290167
©HOME DESIGN SERVICES, INC.

DESIGN FEATURES
BEDROOMS: 4
BATHROOMS: 3½
FIRST FLOOR: 3,770 Sq. Ft.
SECOND FLOOR: 634 Sq. Ft.
TOTAL: 4,404 Sq. Ft.
WIDTH: 87'-0"   DEPTH: 97'-6"

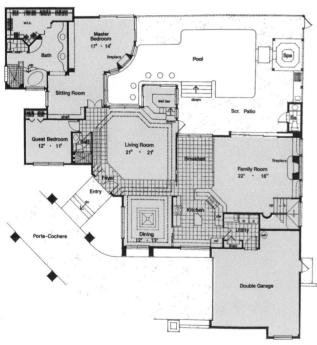

DESIGN FEATURES

BEDROOMS: 4

BATHROOMS: 3½

FIRST FLOOR: 2,669 Sq. Ft.

SECOND FLOOR: 621 Sq. Ft.

TOTAL: 3,290 Sq. Ft.

WIDTH: 78'-0" DEPTH: 84'-6"

DESIGN HPT290168

©HOME DESIGN
SERVICES, INC.

ROOFLINES, ARCHES and corner quoins adorn the facade of this magnificent home. A porte cochere creates a stunning prelude to the double-door entry. A wet bar serves the sunken living room and overlooks the pool area. The dining room has a tray ceiling and is located near the gourmet kitchen with a food-preparation island and angled counter. A guest room opens off the living room. The generous family room, warmed by a fireplace, opens to the screened patio. The master suite provides a sitting room and a fireplace that's set into an angled wall. Its luxurious bath includes a step-up tub. Upstairs, two bedrooms share the oversized balcony and nearby observation room.

DESIGN HPT290169

©ALAN MASCORD DESIGN
ASSOCIATES, INC.

DESIGN FEATURES

BEDROOMS: 3

BATHROOMS: 2½

FIRST FLOOR: 1,820 Sq. Ft.

SECOND FLOOR: 1,384 Sq. Ft.

TOTAL: 3,204 Sq. Ft.

WIDTH: 73'-0" DEPTH: 51'-0"

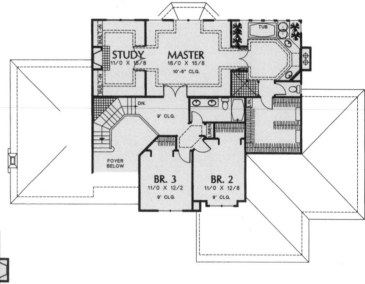

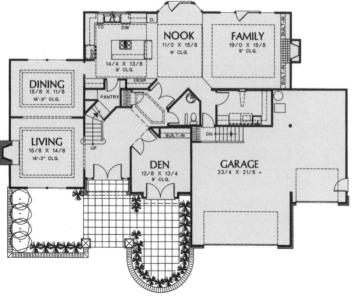

FOR SLIGHTLY SLOPING LOTS, this design puts its best foot forward. From the elegant terraced entry, a great interior unfolds. Formal living and dining rooms dominate the left side of the plan. To the right of the foyer is the private den with front terrace access. A family room is found to the rear, as are the breakfast room and attached island kitchen. Here, an abundance of counter space and a large island cooktop guarantee ease in food preparation. The second floor holds two family bedrooms and an outstanding master suite with its own hearth-warmed study, luxurious bath and immense walk-in closet.

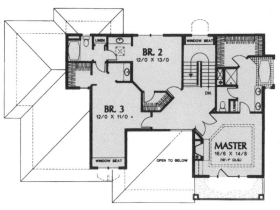

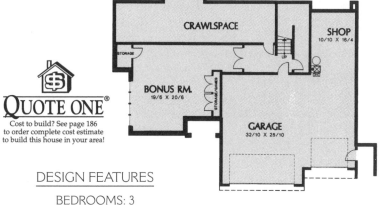

Quote One®

Cost to build? See page 186
to order complete cost estimate
to build this house in your area!

DESIGN FEATURES

BEDROOMS: 3

BATHROOMS: 2½

FIRST FLOOR: 1,989 Sq. Ft.

SECOND FLOOR: 1,349 Sq. Ft.

TOTAL: 3,443 Sq. Ft.

BONUS ROOM: 487 Sq. Ft.

WIDTH: 63'-0" DEPTH: 48'-0"

DESIGN HPT290170
©ALAN MASCORD DESIGN
ASSOCIATES, INC.

DRAMATIC BALCONIES and spectacular window treatments enhance this stunning luxury home. Inside, a through-fireplace warms the formal living room and restful den. Both living spaces open to a balcony that invites quiet reflection on starry nights. The banquet-sized dining room is easily served from the adjacent kitchen. Here, space is shared with an eating nook that provides access to the rear grounds and a family room with a corner fireplace that's perfect for casual gatherings. The upper level contains two family bedrooms and a luxurious master suite that enjoys its own private balcony. The lower level accommodates a shop and a bonus room for future development.

WHEN YOU'RE READY TO ORDER...

Let us show you our blueprint package.

Our Blueprint Package has nearly everything you'll need to get the job done right, with help from an architect, designer, builder or subcontractors. Each set of drawings is the result of many hours of work by licensed architects or professional designers.

QUALITY

Hundreds of hours of painstaking effort have gone into the development of your construction drawings. Each home has been quality-checked by professionals to ensure accuracy and buildability.

VALUE

Because we sell in volume, you can buy professional-quality construction drawings at a fraction of their development cost.

SERVICE

Once you've chosen your favorite home plan, you'll receive fast, efficient service whether you choose to mail or fax your order to us or call us toll free at 1-800-521-6797. **For customer service call toll free 1-888-690-1116.**

SATISFACTION

Over 50 years of service to satisfied home plan buyers provide us unparalleled experience and knowledge in producing quality blueprints. What this means to you is satisfaction with our product and performance.

ORDER TOLL FREE
1-800-521-6797

After you've looked over our Blueprint Package and Important Extras on the following pages, simply mail the order form on page 191 or call toll free on our Order Hotline: 1-800-521-6797. We're ready and eager to serve you.

For customer service, call toll free 1-888-690-1116.

THE BLUEPRINT PACKAGE

Each set of construction drawings is a related gathering of plans, diagrams, measurements, details and specifications that precisely show how your new residence will come together. Each home design receives careful attention and planning from our expert staff to ensure quality and buildability. Set may include:

Frontal Sheet
The artist's sketch of the full exterior of the house provides a projected view of how the home will look when built and landscaped. Large ink-line floor plans show all levels of the house and offer an overview of your new home's livability.

SAMPLE PACKAGE

Foundation Plans

This sheet shows the foundation layout including support walls, excavated and unexcavated areas, if any, and foundation notes.

Detailed Floor Plans

These sheets show the layout of each floor of the house. Rooms and interior spaces are carefully dimensioned and keys are given for cross-section details provided later in the plans. The positions of electrical outlets and switches are shown.

House Cross-Sections

Large-scale views show sections or cut-aways of the foundation, interior walls, exterior walls, floors, stairways and roof details. Additional cross-sections may show important changes in floor, ceiling or roof heights

of the relationship of one level to another. Extremely valuable for construction, these sections show exactly how the various parts of the house fit together.

Interior Elevations

Many of our drawings show the design and placement of kitchen and bathroom cabinets, laundry areas, fireplaces, bookcases and other built-ins. Little "extras," such as mantelpiece and wainscoting drawings, plus moulding sections, provide details that give your home a custom touch.

Exterior Elevations

These drawings show the front, rear and sides of your house and give necessary notes on exterior materials and finishes. Particular attention is given to cornice detail, brick and stone accents or other finish items that make your home unique.

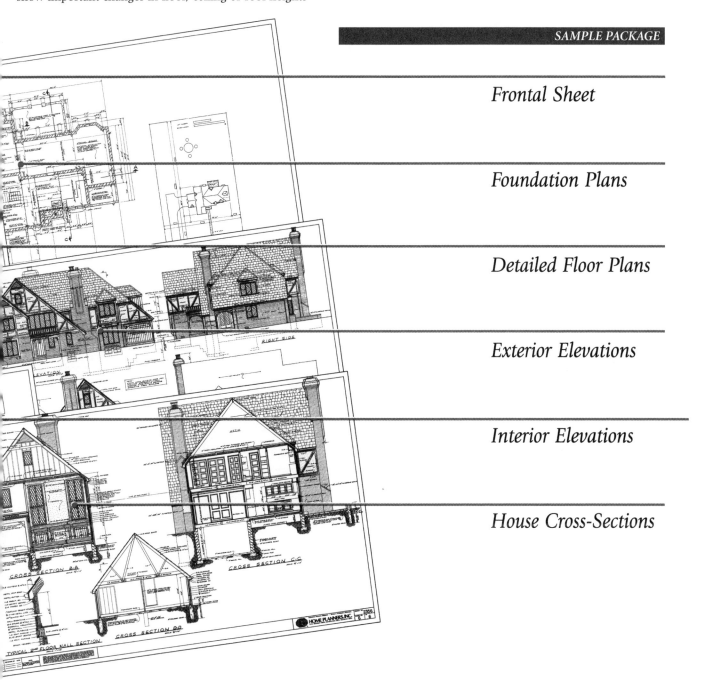

SAMPLE PACKAGE

Frontal Sheet

Foundation Plans

Detailed Floor Plans

Exterior Elevations

Interior Elevations

House Cross-Sections

Important Extras To Do The Job Right!

Introducing eight important planning and construction aids developed by our professionals to help you succeed in your home-building project.

SPECIFICATION OUTLINE

This valuable 16-page document is critical to building your house correctly. Designed to be filled in by you or your builder, this book lists 166 stages or items crucial to the building process. It provides a comprehensive review of the construction process and helps in choosing materials. When combined with the construction drawings, a signed contract, and a schedule, it becomes a legal document and record for the building of your home.

MATERIALS LIST

For many of the designs in our portfolio, we offer a customized materials take-off that is invaluable in planning and estimating the cost of your new home. This Materials List outlines the quantity, type and size of materials needed to build your house (with the exception of mechanical system items). Included are framing lumber, windows and doors, kitchen and bath cabinetry, rough and finish hardware, and much more. This handy list helps you or your builder cost out materials and serves as a reference sheet when you're compiling bids. A Materials List cannot be ordered before construction drawings are ordered.

(Note: Because of the diversity of local building codes, our Materials List does not include mechanical materials.)

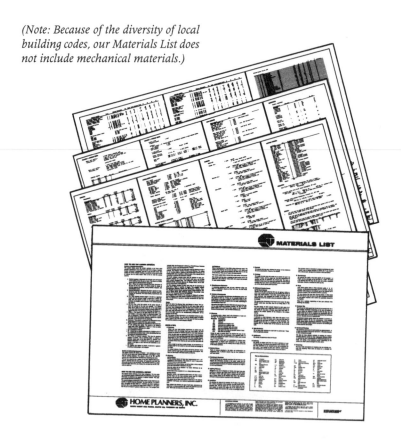

DETAIL SETS

Each set is an excellent tool that will add to your understanding of these technical subjects and help you deal more confidently with subcontractors.

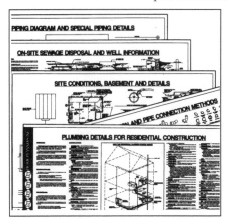

PLUMBING

If you want to know more about the complete plumbing system, these 24x36-inch detail sheets will prove very useful. Prepared to meet requirements of the National Plumbing Code, these six fact-filled sheets give general information on pipe schedules, fittings, sump-pump details, water-softener hookups, septic system details and much more. Color-coded sheets include a glossary of terms.

ELECTRICAL

Prepared to meet requirements of the National Electrical Code, these comprehensive 24x36-inch drawings come packed with helpful information, including wire sizing, switch-installation schematics, cable-routing details, appliance wattage, doorbell hookups, typical service panel circuitry and much more. Six sheets are bound together and color-coded for easy reference.

CONSTRUCTION

To help you understand how your house will be built—and offer additional techniques—this set of drawings depicts the materials and methods used to build foundations, fireplaces, walls, floors and roofs. Where appropriate, the drawings show acceptable alternatives. These six sheets will answer questions for the advanced do-it-yourselfer or home planner.

MECHANICAL

This package will help you make informed decisions and communicate with subcontractors about heating and cooling systems. The 24 x 36-inch drawings contain instructions and samples that allow you to make simple load calculations and preliminary sizing and costing analysis. Covered are today's most commonly used systems from heat pumps to solar fuel systems. The package is full of illustrations and diagrams to help you visualize components and how they relate to one another.

PLAN A HOME®

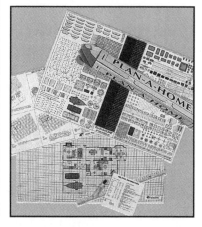

Plan-A-Home® is an easy-to-use tool that helps you design a new home, arrange furniture in a new or existing home, or plan a remodeling project. Each package contains:

- **More than 700 reusable peel-off planning symbols** on a self-stick vinyl sheet including walls, windows, doors, all types of furniture, kitchen components, bath fixtures and many more.

- **A reusable, transparent, ¼-inch scale planning grid** that matches the scale of actual working drawings (¼-inch equals one foot). This grid provides the basis for house layouts of up to 140 x 92 feet.

- **Tracing paper** and a protective sheet for copying or transferring your completed plan.

- **A felt-tip pen,** with water-soluble ink that wipes away.

Plan-A-Home® lets you lay out areas as large as a 7,500 square foot, six-bedroom, seven-bath house.

To Order, Call Toll Free 1-800-521-6797

To add these important extras to your set of construction drawings, indicate your choices on the order form on page 191 or call us toll free at 1-800-521-6797 and we'll tell you more about these exciting products. For customer service, call toll free 1-888-690-1116.

House Plans Price Schedule
Prices guaranteed through December 31, 2001

One-set
Building Package

One set of vellum construction drawings
plus one set of study blueprints @ $.35 / square foot

Eight-set Blueprint Package ....$.30 square foot
Additional Set of Identical Blueprints in same order ....$50 set
(must be ordered within 60 days of original purchase)
Specification Outlines ....$10 each
Materials Lists are available for many designers ....call for pricing

Purchase Policy
Accurate construction-cost estimates should come from your builder after review of the construction drawings. Your purchase includes a license to use the plans to construct one single-family residence. You may not use this design to build a second or derivative work, or construct multiple dwellings without purchasing another set of drawings or paying additional design fees. An additional identical set of the same plan in the same order may be purchased within a 60-day period at $50 per set, plus shipping and sales tax. After 60 days, re-orders are treated as new orders.

Sepias, vellums and other reproducibles are not refundable, returnable or exchangeable.
Reproducible vellums are granted with a non-exclusive license to do the following:

❑ to modify the drawings for use in the construction of a single home.
❑ to make up to twelve (12) copies of the plans for use in the construction of a single home.
❑ to construct one and only one home based on the plans, either in the original form or as modified by you.

Plans were designed to meet the requirements of the local building codes in the jurisdiction for which they were drawn. Because codes are subject to various changes and interpretations, the purchaser is responsible for compliance with all local building codes, ordinances, site conditions, subdivision restrictions and structural elements by having their builder review the plans to ensure compliance. We strongly recommend that an engineer in your area review your plans before you apply for a permit or actual construction begins. We authorize the use of our drawings on the express condition that you strictly comply with all local building codes, zoning requirements and other applicable laws, regulations, ordinances and requirements.

Index

To use the Index at the right, refer to the design number (a helpful page reference is also given). To Order: Fill in and send the order form on page 191 or, if you prefer, fax to 1-800-224-6699 or 520-544-3086 or call toll free 1-800-521-6797 or 520-297-8200.

DESIGN	PRICE	PAGE	MATERIALS LIST	CUSTOMIZABLE	QUOTE ONE	DECK	DECK PRICE	LANDSCAPE	LANDSCAPE PRICE	REGIONS
HPT290001	C2	8								
HPT290002	C2	9								
HPT290003	C2	10	Y							
HPT290004	C4	11								
HPT290005	C3	12	Y		Y					
HPT290006	L2	13	Y							
HPT290007	C4	14	Y							
HPT290008	C1	15	Y							
HPT290009	C4	16	Y							
HPT290010	C4	17	Y		Y					
HPT290011	L4	18								
HPT290012	L1	19	Y	Y		ODA008	P3	OLA016	P4	1234568
HPT290013	C3	20	Y		Y					
HPT290014	C2	21	Y							
HPT290015	C1	22								
HPT290016	L1	23								
HPT290017	C1	24	Y							
HPT290018	C2	25	Y		Y					
HPT290019	C3	26	Y							
HPT290020	C3	27	Y							
HPT290021	C1	28	Y							
HPT290022	C2	29	Y							
HPT290023	C2	30	Y							
HPT290024	A4	31	Y							
HPT290025	C2	32	Y							
HPT290026	C4	34	Y							
HPT290027	C1	35								
HPT290028	C2	36	Y							
HPT290029	C1	37								
HPT290030	C2	38								
HPT290031	C1	39	Y		Y					
HPT290032	A4	40								
HPT290033	C1	41								
HPT290034	C4	42	Y		Y					
HPT290035	C4	43								
HPT290036	L2	44								
HPT290037	L1	45								
HPT290038	C3	46								
HPT290039	C3	47	Y							
HPT290040	A4	48	Y							
HPT290041	L3	49								
HPT290042	C4	50								
HPT290043	L2	51	Y	Y				OLA028	P4	12345678
HPT290044	L1	52								
HPT290045	C2	53	Y							
HPT290046	C2	54								
HPT290047	C4	55								
HPT290048	C4	56								
HPT290049	L1	57	Y	Y						
HPT290050	L2	58								
HPT290051	C1	59								
HPT290052	C4	60	Y							
HPT290053	C3	61								
HPT290054	C2	62								
HPT290055	C1	64	Y							
HPT290056	C2	65								
HPT290057	C2	66	Y	Y		ODA011	P2	OLA024	P4	123568
HPT290058	C2	67	Y	Y	Y			OLA024	P4	123568
HPT290059	A4	68	Y	Y	Y			OLA024	P4	123568
HPT290060	L1	69	Y	Y	Y	ODA012	P3	OLA024	P4	123568
HPT290061	C1	70	Y	Y	Y	ODA011	P2	OLA003	P3	123568
HPT290062	C1	71								
HPT290063	C1	72	Y							
HPT290064	A4	73	Y							
HPT290065	C1	74	Y	Y				OLA024	P4	123568
HPT290066	C4	75	Y	Y		ODA012	P3	OLA024	P4	123568
HPT290067	A4	76	Y							
HPT290068	C1	77	Y							
HPT290069	C3	78	Y	Y				OLA024	P4	123568
HPT290070	C2	79						OLA004	P3	123568
HPT290071	A4	80	Y							
HPT290072	C1	81	Y	Y	Y			OLA010	P3	1234568
HPT290073	C2	82								
HPT290074	L2	84	Y							
HPT290075	C1	85								
HPT290076	C4	86								
HPT290077	C4	87								
HPT290078	C4	88								
HPT290079	L1	89								
HPT290080	C2	90	Y							
HPT290081	C2	91	Y							
HPT290082	C2	92	Y							
HPT290083	L2	93								
HPT290084	C3	94	Y							
HPT290085	L1	95								

DESIGN	PRICE	PAGE	MATERIALS LIST	CUSTOMIZABLE	QUOTE ONE	DECK	DECK PRICE	LANDSCAPE	LANDSCAPE PRICE	REGIONS
HPT290086	C4	96								
HPT290087	C3	97								
HPT290088	L3	98								
HPT290089	C3	99	Y							
HPT290090	C3	100	Y							
HPT290091	C3	101	Y							
HPT290092	C3	102	Y							
HPT290093	C3	103	Y							
HPT290094	C3	104	Y							
HPT290095	C2	105	Y							
HPT290096	C4	106	Y							
HPT290097	C3	107	Y							
HPT290098	C1	108	Y							
HPT290099	C1	109	Y							
HPT290100	A4	110								
HPT290101	C4	111	Y		Y					
HPT290102	C3	112	Y		Y					
HPT290103	C4	113	Y		Y					
HPT290104	L1	114	Y		Y					
HPT290105	C3	115	Y							
HPT290106	C3	116	Y							
HPT290107	C3	117	Y							
HPT290108	C3	118								
HPT290109	C3	120	Y	Y	Y			OLA037	P4	347
HPT290110	C2	121	Y	Y	Y			OLA034	P3	347
HPT290111	C4	122	Y	Y	Y					
HPT290112	C1	123	Y		Y			OLA038	P3	7
HPT290113	C1	124	Y	Y	Y			OLA014	P4	12345678
HPT290114	C1	125	Y	Y	Y			OLA038	P3	7
HPT290115	C1	126	Y	Y	Y			OLA034	P3	347
HPT290116	C4	127	Y	Y						
HPT290117	C3	128						OLA012	P3	12345678
HPT290118	C3	129				ODA011	P2	OLA012	P3	12345678
HPT290119	C2	130						OLA012	P3	12345678
HPT290120	A4	131								
HPT290121	C3	132	Y		Y			OLA001	P3	123568
HPT290122	C4	133	Y					OLA017	P3	123568
HPT290123	C4	134								
HPT290124	C2	135								
HPT290125	C3	136	Y					OLA008	P4	1234568
HPT290126	C1	137								
HPT290127	C1	138						OLA024	P4	123568
HPT290128	C2	139	Y		Y			OLA024	P4	123568
HPT290129	L1	140	Y		Y			OLA037	P4	347
HPT290130	L1	142								
HPT290131	L3	143								
HPT290132	C3	144	Y							
HPT290133	C4	145								
HPT290134	C3	146	Y							
HPT290135	C3	147								
HPT290136	L1	148						OLA017	P3	123568
HPT290137	C3	149	Y							
HPT290138	C3	150	Y							
HPT290139	C4	151								
HPT290140	C1	152								
HPT290141	C2	153								
HPT290142	A4	154	Y		Y					
HPT290143	A4	155	Y		Y					
HPT290144	C2	156								
HPT290145	C2	157								
HPT290146	C3	158								
HPT290147	C3	159	Y							
HPT290148	L1	160	Y		Y					
HPT290149	C2	161	Y							
HPT290150	C3	162						OLA005	P3	123568
HPT290151	A4	164	Y							
HPT290152	C1	165	Y							
HPT290153	L1	166								
HPT290154	C3	167								
HPT290155	C4	168								
HPT290156	L1	169								
HPT290157	C3	170								
HPT290158	L1	171								
HPT290159	C2	172								
HPT290160	C2	173								
HPT290161	C2	174	Y					OLA001	P3	123568
HPT290162	C2	175	Y					OLA001	P3	123568
HPT290163	C2	176	Y					OLA001	P3	123568
HPT290164	C2	177	Y					OLA004	P3	123568
HPT290165	L1	178								
HPT290166	C2	179	Y					OLA004	P3	123568
HPT290167	L1	180								
HPT290168	C2	181								
HPT290169	C2	182	Y							
HPT290170	C3	183	Y		Y					

Before You Order...

Before filling out the coupon at the right or calling us on our Toll-Free Order Hotline, you may want to learn more about our services and products. Here's some information you will find helpful.

Quick Turnaround
We process and ship every order from our office within two business days. Because of this quick turnaround, we won't send a formal notice acknowledging receipt of your order.

Our Exchange Policy
Sepias, vellums and other reproducibles are not refundable, returnable or exchangeable. Since construction drawings are printed in response to your order, we cannot honor requests for refunds.

Revising, Modifying and Customizing Plans
The wide variety of designs available in this publication allows you to select ideas and concepts for a home to fit your building site and match your family's needs, wants and budget. Like many homeowners who buy these plans, you and your builder, architect or engineer may want to make changes to them. Your builder may make some minor changes, but we recommend that a licensed architect or engineer make most changes. As set forth below, we cannot assume any responsibility for construction drawings that have been changed, whether by you, your builder or by professionals selected by you or referred to you by us, because such individuals are outside our supervision and control.

Architectural and Engineering Seals
Some cities and states are now requiring that a licensed architect or engineer review and "seal" a blueprint or construction drawing and officially approve it prior to construction due to concerns over energy costs, safety and other factors. Prior to application for a building permit or the start of actual construction, we strongly advise you to consult your local building official who can tell you if such a review is required.

Local Building Codes and Zoning Requirements
Each plan was designed to meet the requirements of the local building codes in the jurisdiction for which they were drawn. Because building codes change from time to time and are subject to various interpretations, plans may not comply with any such code at the time they are sold to a customer. In addition, building officials may not accept these plans as final construction documents of record as the plans may need to be modified and additional drawings and details added to suit local conditions and requirements. We strongly advise purchasers to consult a licensed architect or engineer and their local building official before starting any construction related to these plans or applying for any permit. Your plan may need to be modified to comply with local requirements regarding snow loads, energy codes, soil and seismic conditions and a wide range of other matters. In addition, you may need to obtain permits or inspections from local governments before and in the course of construction. The purchaser is responsible for compliance with all the local building codes, ordinances, site conditions, subdivision restrictions and structural elements by having a licensed architect or engineer review the plans to ensure compliance. We authorize the use of our drawings on the express condition that you strictly comply with all local building codes, zoning requirements and other applicable laws, regulations, ordinances and requirements. **Notice: Plans for homes to be built in Nevada must be re-drawn by a Nevada-registered professional.** Consult your building official for more information on this subject.

Foundation and Exterior Wall Changes
Most of our plans are drawn with a basement foundation. Most professional contractors and builders can easily adapt your plans to alternate foundation types.

Disclaimer
We have put substantial care and effort into the creation of our construction drawings. However, because we cannot provide on-site consultation, supervision and control over actual construction, and because of the great variance in local building requirements, building practices and soil, seismic, weather and other conditions, WE CANNOT MAKE ANY WARRANTY, EXPRESS OR IMPLIED, WITH RESPECT TO THE CONTENT OR USE OF OUR CONSTRUCTION DRAWINGS OR BLUEPRINTS, INCLUDING BUT NOT LIMITED TO ANY WARRANTY OF MERCHANTABILITY OR OF FITNESS FOR A PARTICULAR PURPOSE. **ITEMS, PRICES, TERMS AND CONDITIONS ARE SUBJECT TO CHANGE WITHOUT NOTICE. REPRODUCIBLE PLAN ORDERS MAY REQUIRE A CUSTOMER'S SIGNED RELEASE BEFORE SHIPPING ORDER.**

Terms and Conditions
These designs are protected under the terms of United States Copyright Law and may not be copied or reproduced in any way, by any means, unless you have purchased sepias or reproducibles which clearly indicate your right to copy or reproduce. We authorize the use of your chosen design as an aid in the construction of one single family home only. You may not use this design to build a second or multiple dwellings without purchasing another set of drawings or paying additional design fees.

Have You Seen Our Newest Designs?

Home Planners is one of the country's most active home design firms, creating nearly 100 new plans each year. At least 50 of our latest creations are featured in each edition of our New Design Portfolio. You may have received a copy with your latest purchase by mail. If not, or if you purchased this book from a local retailer, just return the coupon below for your FREE copy. Make sure you consider the very latest of what Home Planners has to offer.

Yes! Please send my FREE copy of your latest New Design Portfolio.

Offer good to U.S. shipping address only.

Name _____

Address _____

City _____ State _____ Zip _____

HOME PLANNERS, LLC
Wholly owned by Hanley-Wood, LLC
3275 WEST INA ROAD, SUITE 110
TUCSON, ARIZONA 85741

Order Form Key

| HPT29 |

OR: copy the Order Form on page 191 and send it via our FAX line: 1-800-224-6699.

The Home Customizer®

"This house is perfect...if only the family room were two feet wider." Sound familiar? In response to the numerous requests for this type of modification, Home Planners has developed **The Home Customizer® Package**. This exclusive package offers our top-of-the-line materials to make it easy for anyone, anywhere to customize any Home Planners design to fit their needs. Check the index on page 189 for those plans which are customizable.

Some of the changes you can make to any of our plans include:

- exterior elevation changes
- kitchen and bath modifications
- roof, wall and foundation changes
- room additions and more!

The Home Customizer® Package includes everything you'll need to make the necessary changes to your favorite Home Planners design. The package includes:

- instruction book with examples
- architectural scale and clear work film
- erasable red marker and removable correction tape
- ¼"-scale furniture cutouts
- 1 set reproducible drawings
- 1 set study blueprints for communicating changes to your design professional
- a copyright release letter so you can make copies as you need them
- referral letter with the name, address and telephone number of the professional in your region who is trained in modifying Home Planners designs efficiently and inexpensively.

The Home Customizer® Package will not only save you 25% to 75% of the cost of drawing the plans from scratch with an architect or engineer, it will also give you the flexibility to have your changes and modifications made by our referral network or by the professional of your choice. Now it's even easier and more affordable to have the custom home you've always wanted.

ORDER TOLL FREE!
For information about any of our services or to order call
1-800-521-6797 or
520-297-8200
Browse our website:
www.eplans.com

> **SEPIAS, VELLUMS AND OTHER REPRODUCIBLES ARE NOT REFUNDABLE, RETURNABLE OR EXCHANGEABLE.**

For Customer Service, call toll free 1-888-690-1116

HOME PLANNERS, LLC
Wholly owned by Hanley-Wood, LLC
®3275 WEST INA ROAD, SUITE 110
TUCSON, ARIZONA 85741

THE BASIC PACKAGE
Rush me the following (Please refer to the Plans Index and Price Schedule on pages 188-189):
One-Set Building Package for Plan Number(s)@ $.35/sq. ft._____. $_____
___ Eight-set Blueprint Package @$.30/sq. ft._____. $_____
___ Additional Identical Blueprints in same order @$50 per set $_____

ADDITIONAL PRODUCTS
Rush me the following:
___ Plan-A-Home® @ $29.95 ea. $_____
___ Specification Outlines @ $10 each. $_____
___ Materials List call for pricing and availability. $_____
___ Home Customizer Kit @ $50 each. $_____
___ Detail Sets @$14.95 each; any two for $22.95; any three
for $29.95; all four for $39.95 (Save $19.85). $_____
  ___Plumbing___Electrical___Construction___Mechanical
(These helpful details provide general construction advice and
are not specific to any single plan.)

POSTAGE AND HANDLING	1-3 sets	4 or more sets
Signature is required for all deliveries.		
Delivery: (No COD's)		
(Requires street address—No P.o. Boxes)		
• Regular Service (Allow 7-10 business days delivery)	$20.00	$25.00
• Priority (Allow 4-5 business days delivery)	$25.00	$35.00
• Express (Allow 3 business days delivery)	$35.00	$45.00

OVERSEAS DELIVERY: Fax, phone or mail for quote.

NOTE: All delivery times are from date Construction Drawings are shipped.

POSTAGE (From box above) $_____
SUB TOTAL $_____
SALES TAX (AZ & MI residents
        please add appropriate state & local sales tax.) $_____
TOTAL (Sub total and Tax) $_____

YOUR ADDRESS (Please print legibly)
Name _____

Street _____

City_____State_____Zip_____

Daytime telephone number (required) (_____) _____

FOR CREDIT CARD ORDERS ONLY
Please fill in the information below:
Credit card number _____

Exp. Date: Month/Year _____
Check one ❒ Visa   ❒ MasterCard   ❒ Discover   ❒ American Express

Signature (required)_____
Please check appropriate box: ❒ Licensed Builder-Contractor
                                ❒ Homeowner

BY FAX: Copy the order form above and send it on our
FAXLINE: **1-800-224-6699 or 1-520-544-3086**

Order Form Key

> HPT29

ABOUT *the* DESIGNERS

ALAN MASCORD DESIGN ASSOCIATES, INC.

Founded in 1983 as a local supplier to the building community, Mascord Design Associates of Portland, Oregon began to successfully publish plans nationally in 1985. The company's trademark is creating floor plans that work well and exhibit excellent traffic patterns.

ARCHIVAL DESIGNS, INC.

David Marc Loftus of Archival Designs, Inc. has celebrated fifteen years in the residential design business. His firm has been growing at an accelerated rate because his designs reflect the collective wisdom of the past. His award-winning style is called "Classic Traditional."

BRELAND & FARMER DESIGNERS, INC.

Designer Edsel Breland is owner and president of Breland & Farmer Designers, Inc., which he founded in 1973. The homes designed by Breland have a definite Southern signature, but fit perfectly in any region.

DESIGN BASICS, INC.

For nearly a decade, Design Basics, a nationally recognized home design service located in Omaha, Nebraska, has been developing plans for custom home builders. Since 1987, the firm has consistently appeared in *Builder* magazine, the official magazine of the National Association of Home Builders, as one of the top-selling designers.

DONALD A. GARDNER ARCHITECTS, INC.

The South Carolina firm of Donald A. Gardner was established in response to a growing demand for residential designs that reflect constantly changing lifestyles. The company's specialty is providing homes with refined, custom-style details and unique features such as passive-solar designs and open floor plans.

ERIC S. BROWN DESIGN GROUP, INC.

Eric Brown's philosophy is that artistry and technology meld into the ideal living space. His perspective embraces classic structures of the past, but is responsive to evolving lifestyles of today. He advocates attention to every element in design, resulting in award-winning, comprehensive homes.

FILLMORE DESIGN GROUP

Fillmore Design Group was formed in 1960 in Oklahoma City, Oklahoma by Robert L. Fillmore, president and founder. "Our designs are often characterized by their European influence, by massive brick gables and by high-flowing, graceful rooflines," says Fillmore.

FRANK BETZ ASSOCIATES, INC.

Frank Betz Associates, Inc., located in Smyrna, Georgia, is one of the nation's leaders in the design of stock plans. FBA, Inc. has provided builders and developers with home plans since 1977.

HOME DESIGN SERVICES, INC.

Home Design Services is a full-service design firm that has specialized in residential and multi-family design for thirty years. The firm offers a full complement of services, taking a project from concept through completed construction documents. The company's vast experience provides a considerable knowledge of current design trends.

HOME PLANNERS

Headquartered in Tucson, Arizona, with additional offices in Detroit, Home Planners is one of the longest-running and most successful home design firms in the United States. With over 2,500 designs in its portfolio, the company provides a wide range of styles, sizes and types of homes for the residential builder.

LARRY E. BELK DESIGNS

Through the years, Larry E. Belk has worked with individuals and builders alike to provide a quality product. Flowing, open spaces and interesting angles define his interiors. Great emphasis is placed on providing views that showcase the natural environment.

LARRY JAMES & ASSOCIATES, INC.

Larry James has been designing classic homes since 1972. His goal is to create a collection of timeless designs. He likes to design new homes that trigger pleasant memories of times-gone-by—"Twenty-first-century living wrapped in a turn-of-the-century package" is Larry's design philosophy. He strives to design beautiful homes that will never fade.

LIVING CONCEPTS HOME PLANNING

With more than twenty years of design experience, Living Concepts Home Planning has built an outstanding reputation for its many award-winning residential designs. Based in Charlotte, North Carolina, the company was founded by partners Frank Snodgrass, Chris Boush, Kim Bunting and Derik Boush. Because of its affinity for glass and designs that take full advantage of outside views, Living Concepts specializes in homes for golf and lakefront communities.

THE SATER DESIGN COLLECTION, INC.

The Sater Design Collection has a long established tradition of providing South Florida's most diverse and extraordinary custom designed homes. This is exemplified by over 50 national design awards, numerous magazine features and, most important, satisfied clients.

STEPHEN FULLER, INC.

Stephen S. Fuller established his design group with the tenets of innovation, quality, originality and uncompromising architectural techniques in traditional and European homes. Especially popular throughout the Southeast, Stephen Fuller's plans are known for their extensive detail and thoughtful design.